저자 김선태 목사 드립니다.

Rev. Sun Foe Kim

The Boy in Search of Heaven's Light

THE TRUE STORY OF SUNTAE KIM

The Boy in Search of Heaven's Light
THE TRUE STORY OF SUNTAE KIM

Copyright©2012 by Suntae Kim
Published by Word of Life Press
Songwoldong #32-43, Jongnogu, Seoul 110-102 Korea

Original Autobiography *River of Hope* by Rev. Suntae Kim
Adapted by Mihyeong Kim
Translated & Edited by John-Francis Kinsler, Yuna Jeong & Jongwon Oh
Design & Layout by Kyunghee Lee
Illustration SeungAe Lee

Printed in Korea

The Boy in Search
of Heaven's Light
THE TRUE STORY OF SUNTAE KIM

ⓒ 김선태 2012

2012년 7월 28일 1판 1쇄 발행

펴낸이 | 김창영
펴낸곳 | 생명의말씀사

등록 | 1962. 1. 10. No.300-1962-1
주소 | 서울 종로구 송월동 32-43(110-101)
전화 | 02)738-6555(본사) · 02)3159-7979(영업)
팩스 | 02)739-3824(본사) · 080-022-8585(영업)

지은이 | 김선태

기획편집 | John-Francis Kinsler, 정유나, 오종원
글 | 김미영
디자인 | 이경희
일러스트 | 이승애
인쇄 | 영진문원
제본 | 정문바인텍

ISBN 978-89-04-16144-7 (03230)

The Boy in Search
of Heaven's Light
THE TRUE STORY OF SUNTAE KIM

Word of
Life
Press

The Boy in Search of Heaven's Light

THE TRUE STORY OF SUNTAE KIM

CONTENTS

Part 4 Sailing on the Wings of Hope

Part 5 Conclusion

And Jesus said to him, "If you can! All things are possible for one who believes."

Mark 9:23

Introduction

Blind since he was ten years old, Suntae Kim had to exert ten times as much effort as the next person to live normally in a society where the handicapped were not considered a productive part of the community. But not only did he overcome a widespread prejudice in Korea that treated the disabled as a curse and a burden, he surpassed many other individuals who had full use of their eyes to become an educated pastor, healer, and leader.

Overcoming personal grief and tragedy is only one part of the unique story of Suntae Kim's life. The other part is helping hundreds of thousands of Koreans — either blind or low-visioned — to regain their sight or acquire opportunities for education and employment. As a force for good, Kim has led many lives to God. At the same time, he has strongly influenced society to attend to the needs of the blind and reverse the very attitude that almost made him a victim.

His faith in Christ is at the root of both successes. Korea's first blind minister credits his faith for lifting him up in his darkest hours and for giving him a vision of his ministry. In an autobiography entitled *River of Hope* (2001), Reverend Kim says, "If I had never resolved the pain I received through poverty, discrimination and many abuses, my heart would have languished in hatred toward the whole world throughout my life."

For a blind orphan who had to struggle with extraordinary adversities to find his way in the world, the achievement of Suntae Kim is phenomenal. He has not only pioneered in establishing churches for the blind in South Korea, he founded pioneering medical and welfare institutions that have improved the quality of life for the visually handicapped. From 1995 to the first half of 2004, for instance, Siloam Eye Hospital provided free treatment and operations to 23,806 and 3,933 patients, respectively. During the same period, the Mobile Eye Hospital provided free treatment to 103,207 and free operations to 4,625 persons. Impressive as these figures are, they tell only part of Kim's story.

For the blind minister, juggling the financial concerns of the Siloam Foundation, Siloam Eye Hospital, and the various institutions for the blind that he is connected with has not posed an insurmountable problem. Nor has success changed anything of the Christian character he had developed through his early years of suffering.

He continues to donate all the money he receives to his ministry. At sevsenty, Kim lives a simple life in Seoul with his wife and three daughters. He remains perfectly healthy, jogging up the mountain daily and continuing to teach at the Presbyterian College and Theological Seminary and at the Soongsil and Han Il universities where he is an adjunct professor. The fifteen-hour workday he keeps is as much a reflection of his devotion to his ministry as to his Christian faith.

"I believed that God would bless me if I lived a faithful life. Because I had learned to live a diligent life since I was small, I try my best to live more diligently than anyone else," he says. Here is the amazing story of the young Suntae Kim who grew into a hero and role-model for many around the world.

Alex Dacanay
Ramon Magsaysay Award Foundation
2011

2007 Ramon Magsaysay
Award for Public Service

Award Citation for
Suntae Kim:

It is a cruel fate anywhere to be blind, and all the more cruel in societies where sightless people are cursed as unlucky and shamed as useless burdens on their families and on society at large. Suntae Kim, director of Seoul's Siloam Eye Hospital, knows these degrading aspects of Korean society from bitter personal experience. He has devoted his life to changing them.

Kim Suntae was not born blind. For the first ten years of his life, he was the adored only son of a prosperous family. In June 1950, the violent outbreak of the Korean War suddenly rendered him an orphan. Not long afterwards, a mortar shell that he and other boys found while scavenging for food exploded and left him blind. Even his own relatives now treated him like a pariah and a slave. He ran away. Learning to survive as a beggar, Kim gathered strength from the random kindnesses of compassionate Koreans and American soldiers, and from Christian teachings he had imbibed in Sunday school.

"God, please help me," he prayed.

Kim persevered and developed an iron will. From the hard life of the streets, he moved to the hard life of wartime orphanages and finally into school. He learned to read Korean Braille and to type. Vowing to become a Christian pastor, he became the first blind graduate of Seoul's

Soongsil High School and, in 1962, overcame the resistance of Korea's military junta to enter Soongsil University. A master's degree in theology followed in 1969, a doctorate in 1993.

Meeting hardship with frugality, Kim struggled to form Korea's first church for the blind in 1972. Its seven members worshipped in a borrowed room and a dilapidated apartment. The following year, the Presbyterian Church of Korea named Kim director of Blind Evangelical Missions, a new department with a staff of one. He seized the opportunity to build a ministry for blind Christians, visiting church after church, publishing Braille bibles and hymnals, and launching a scholarship program for deserving students.

He began to travel widely and, in Japan and the United States, witnessed public amenities and rehabilitation programs for the blind that enlarged his hopes for Korea.

Increasingly, Kim devoted himself to the dream of a hospital dedicated to treating and curing blindness. Drawing support from Korea's business community, in 1986 he led in founding Siloam Eye Hospital, where sight-restoring surgery and state-of-the-art facilities were available free to the needy. In 1996, Kim added a mobile clinic to deliver eye services to the rural poor, prison inmates, and other underserved communities. And, in 1997, he opened Korea's largest rehabilitation-and-learning center to help blind and low-vision people cope with day-to-day life, learn new job skills, and become computer-literate using new Braille-and voice-friendly software. Meanwhile, Kim's voice and esteemed example helped advance new laws requiring safe public spaces and employment for the disabled.

Today, more than twenty thousand people have received free eye surgery and two hundred thousand more have been treated at Siloam Eye Hospital and its mobile unit. There are medical missions to Bangladesh, Kenya, China, and the Philippines. And nearly one thousand students have received scholarships through programs that Kim initiated.

Moreover, the church for the blind that he founded thirty-five years ago now has its own sanctuary, four hundred members, and many vibrant offshoots and branches.

As for his own role in all of this, Kim echoes the words of the Apostle Paul, "I can do all things through Him who gives me strength."

But Pastor Kim also has some words of his own. He says, "Blessed are those who never give up."

In electing Suntae Kim to receive the 2007 Ramon Magsaysay Award for Public Service, the board of trustees recognizes his inspiring ministry of hope and practical assistance to his fellow blind and visually impaired citizens in South Korea.

Ramon Magsaysay Award Presentation Ceremonies
Manila, Philippines
31 August 2007

Translator's Note

Although Rev. Kim's first name is romanized as Sun-Tae Kim,
this book is geared for a young English speaking audience perhaps
unfamiliar with hyphenated asian names, and so his is referred to
throughout the book as Suntae Kim.

Part 1
To Lose
Everything

Chapter 1

Remembrance of
My Hometown

"Suntae," said grandmother. "Are you on your way to church again?"

Since she found out that Suntae had been sneaking out to church secretly, she kept saying the same things to scold him.

"Christians bring bad luck to their family. You should never go to church again."

Suntae was born into a wealthy family with a strong faith in Buddhism who ran a clothing business. All of the family members, father, mother, grandmother, and Suntae were strong believers in Buddhism. Even on the day Suntae was born, Grandma made her way to the Buddhist temple with the new-born baby in her arms and prayed to Buddha to bless her new grandson.

Suntae was a little boy who was always in trouble with his parents because he went out to play with his friends until late. All day long with his friends, Suntae swam around a small island near Seoul, named 'Ttuksom.' Although Suntae's parents would get angry at him often, Suntae was nothing but a big sweetie to his grandma. She always took Suntae's side whenever his parents tried to punish him. Suntae had an aunt, too. Every once in a while, she came back to Suntae's home and adored him. However, strangely enough, grandmother scolded him with great anger every time Suntae tried to go to church. "Are you thinking of going to church tomorrow? Don't even think about it" said grandma strongly. That became a Saturday routine.

The more furious grandma became, the more strongly Suntae wanted to go to church. Strangely, Suntae didn't want to listen to grandma. Maybe it's because he couldn't forget the unforgettable feeling he had on his first day at church.

One day when he was in second grade, one friend said, "Suntae, why don't you come to church with me tomorrow?"

"Church? I don't know"

At that time, he had no idea what church was all about.

"You should come to church. You can eat eggs on Easter Day and rice cake on Christmas. What do you say?"

"Why do they give out all the yummy food for free?" Suntae became curious.

"Why not go? Let's give it a try tomorrow."

So Suntae went to church for delicious treats. When he heard the following hymn for the first time, he found the words quite pleasant and warm. Children gathered around and sang a wonderful hymn.

This is my Father's world,
And to my listening ears,
All nature sings, and round me rings
The music of the spheres.
This is my Father's world:
I rest me in the thought
Of rocks and trees, of skies and seas;
His hand the wonders wrought.

This is my Father's world,
The birds their carols raise

The beautiful chorus opened up Suntae's mind. And, there was one more thing. All the stories he heard during the pastor's sermon were so new and interesting.

Those stories were even more interesting than Grandmother's bedtime stories. He found everything about church touching his soul. The Sunday School teacher asked his name and wrote his name in the attendance book. She patted him on his back, saying "Hope to see you on every Sunday."

Was it the warm affection he felt? Even though he didn't know what it meant to meet the Father and His son Jesus, he went to church every Sunday. As his love for church grew, Grandmother pushed him harder not to go to church, and that only made him want to go even more. One day, he thought deeply, 'How can I go there again?' and Suntae suddenly remembered what pastor had said the other day. "If you pray to the living God, He will make everything come true." So Suntae started to pray, "God! Please make my grandmother die soon." He was indeed a clueless kid who just wanted to go to church without getting in trouble. Maybe was it because of his prayer? Suntae's grandmother, who had stomachaches every once in a while, suddenly passed away when he was in third grade.

Little Suntae thought that he could now make his way to church with no one stopping him. However, at the same time, he was sad as he could no longer see his grandmother again.

Suntae's father dressed his little son in funeral clothes. Whenever new mourners visited his home, his father made Suntae hold a tall stick and weep after him. Nevertheless, little Suntae got so bored and tired of standing there all day that he sneaked out to his friend's house and played. One day after grandmother's funeral, his parents said, "Suntae, Grandmother passed away because of you. You broke her heart by going to church." His parents made him vow that he would not go to church anymore. Suntae promised not to, seeing how firmly their mind was set, but he didn't back down a bit. Even after that day, Suntae went to church and worshipped God behind their backs. Apart from lying to his parents, Suntae was a happy and innocent boy.

Especially because there were so many exciting things in his neighborhood of Shin Dang Dong, located near Ttuksom. In summer, the fruit farms in Ttuksom were full of watermelons, cucumbers, and other delicious summer fruits.

"Mister Farmer, can I eat this melon?"

"Eat as much as you want."

"Mister Farmer, is it okay to have a watermelon?"

"It's all yours." And the farmers used to give him sweet watermelons as big as a soccer ball.

Every summer Suntae and his friends picked watermelons and chilled them in the river. The little kids swam, and ate them when they got hungry. From time to time, he saw farmers from rural towns heading to Seoul with heavy carts full of fruits and vegetables to sell. As a kind boy, Suntae used to help them by pushing the cart from behind. Then farmers used to give him cucumbers and fruits as a token of appreciation.

Suntae used to play outside with his gang of friends all day long until the sun set. In spring, he climbed up mountains and dug out kudzu root. In fall, he picked up beans fallen on the ground after harvesting. In winter, a warm-hearted woman selling hotcakes on the street gave out her hotcakes to Suntae and his friends. With these warm-hearted neighbors, Suntae was truly happy everyday.

Chapter 2

The Terrible Korean War

Suntae started his day like any other day. All of a sudden, the peaceful city of Seoul was turned into a sea of fire as bombs suddenly fell from the sky. There were dead bodies all over the street. Children who had lost their parents were crying and shouting, "Mom, I'm hungry!" or "Mom where are you?"

That was not everything. Suntae witnessed heartless selfish mothers who abandoned their babies. He even saw clearly with his two eyes that some mothers even buried their babies alive and ran away quickly. As Suntae could not understand why such horrible things were happening, his father had to explain to him that war had just broken out. Day and night, Suntae could hear the terrible sounds of airplanes and bombs. When it became quiet, the whole town was destroyed by fire. That was how the Korean War started on June 25th, 1950.

It was about ten days after the war had broken out.

"Suntae, let's eat breakfast," called his father.

"Suntae, you must be more careful because the bombing is getting worse. You must always stay near the house when you play with your friends. Also you must avoid dangerous games. Do you understand me?" said his dad in a concerned voice.

However, Suntae was too young to understand the seriousness of war. Also, curious Suntae could not avoid the temptation to go around the neighborhood to explore new exciting things. Everyday, he would venture out to the next town and when his adventure was over, he spent even more time playing in Ttuksom with his friends.

It was another day in his great adventure. During breakfast, his father told Suntae to be careful as usual, but he went to Ttuksom again to play with his friends. He did not imagine that it would be his last breakfast with his parents.

"I am so hungry. I can't stand it anymore."

Suntae missed eating watermelons from farms. Now the war had made it all impossible. When he was playing with his friends, he forgot all about hunger, however, at one point Suntae could not bear it anymore.

"I am so hungry. Let's stop playing and go home," suggested Suntae.

All the other children were hungry so they all agreed to head back to home. "Sure. Let's go home and have dinner. We can have fun tomorrow."

Suntae was so hungry that even before he turned the corner to his house he started shouting, "Mom! I am starving!" However, Suntae became speechless when he turned the corner.

"Oh! My house should be here! My house should be here after this corner!"

Suntae desperately searched around but he could not find his house. His house was bombed and turned into ashes — only some little traces of the house were left.

Suddenly, Suntae could not breathe. His body was paralyzed with a terrifying horror that could not be described.

He suddenly became an orphan just like the one he saw on the street the other day. Suntae started to cry loudly shouting with all his strength, "Mom! Dad!"

He ran all over the town, but he could not hear any answer from his parents. All his neighbors were destroyed from the bomb too, so Suntae had no place to go. He waited for several days where his house used to be, nevertheless, his parents did not show up after all. They had passed away from the bombing.

Suntae no longer had his parents and home, and he starved for several days. The only way to survive was to beg for food.

"Please, give me something to eat. Please give me some rice," begged Suntae knocking on the door of every house he could find. However, most people had already fled South and the houses were empty. Even worse, some house gardens were full of dead bodies. Because of the extreme situation, Suntae was only able get just enough food to survive through the days. Moreover, it was not easy to sleep at night. He slept under any house's straw roof in summer and he could not get any sleep because of mosquito bites.

Suntae spent his hot summer as a beggar. One summer day, he met some of his friends who had played together at Ttuksom.

They suggested, "Suntae, there are some cucumbers and watermelons farms that are not bombed. Why don't we go and eat?"

"Really? But what if we get caught?"

Suntae was really tempted by his hunger, but at the same time he was worried.

"Come on! We are at war. The owner must've run away. Don't worry and just follow us."

Although Suntae was anxious, he was too hungry to say no. When they arrived at the farm, everyone started eating fruit really fast without hesitation. A few minutes later, one of the friends from the other side of the farm asked the others to check out what he had found. All the boys gathered around the mysterious object. Usually Suntae would be the first one to explore, however, he was too hungry to care at that time.

As Suntae was stuffing his mouth with fruit, he got curious about what his friends were looking at. As he turned his face towards them, Suntae suddenly heard a loud explosion and then lost consciousness.

"Hey. Little boy are you okay? Thank God you are alive. All of your friends died from the bomb explosion but you survived. God helped you."

He heard the voice of a lady near him.

Yet Suntae was confused and puzzled.

As he was getting up to find out what just happened to his friends, he was suddenly paralyzed with shock. He could not see the familiar blue sky and the Han River. All he could see was darkness.

'Is it night already?' thought Suntae, but strangely he could hear the lady but could not see her at all.

What happened to Suntae? When the bomb exploded Suntae was thrown into the air by the force of the blast. As he fell back to the ground, shrapnel and gun powder damaged his eyes and left him blind. The Korean War took away everything from Suntae. He lost his parents, house and most importantly—his eyesight. The summer sunlight was painful for blind Suntae to endure. Even worse, he had lost so much blood that he suffered more from thirst than from hunger. Suntae desperately shouted for help, "Please give me some water! Someone please help me!" He shouted and begged, but nobody was kind enough to give him some water. For people, a blind little boy like Suntae was no big deal.

At that time people had a difficult enough time taking care of themselves and struggling to survive the war.

Suntae had no choice. He crawled on the ground and tried to search for any food and drink with his hands. He ate grass from the ground and even drank muddy water in the rice fields.

'How am I suppose to live from now on?'

'Will I be able to see again?'

'Who can help me?'

Suntae tried to figure out how to survive by asking many questions. Then, he remembered his aunt who used to welcome him with so much love when she visited Suntae's grandmother.

'Okay, if I go to my aunt's house she will help me to see again and educate me. She will take care of me like my own parents,' thought Suntae. The thought of meeting with his aunt gave Suntae courage and hope to live.

Chapter 3

In Search of
His Aunt

Suntae had to cross a big river to go to his aunt's house in Yangju. The bridge had been bombed out long before, so people had to cross by boat. For blind Suntae the journey to his aunt house was not easy at all. Plus, the road to Yangju City was extremely dangerous from bombings.

Nevertheless, Suntae didn't stop on his trip through the river and mountains. Fleeing to Yangju to meet his aunt was the only way for him to survive.

The two bridges crossing the river had been already collapsed because of the bombing. Still so many people were fighting to cross the river to save their lives. The river was just like a brutal battle field. People pushed each other into the river and some drowned. In order to get to the other side of the river, people even stepped on others, whoever was blocking their way. It was impossible to cross during daytime because of the airplane bombing. Only at night people quietly crossed the river on small boats. There were so many people yelling and complaining that they did not get to ride in the boat even though they paid the fare. Suntae was penniless and he did not know what to do in the middle of this awful crisis.

'How can I get on that boat? That boat is the only way to my aunt's house,' he thought.

Suntae could not tell his worries to anyone.

Then he had a great idea. The boat leaves at night so people would not be able to see clearly in the darkness. Also people would be busy carrying their big heavy luggage onto the boat. So he believed people wouldn't notice a skinny little boy like Suntae hiding behind the bags. Suntae found a bag bigger than his body and stayed down quietly between the bags till the boat reached the other side. Although it was against his own idea of right and wrong, it was the only way to get to his aunt's house. He had barely managed to cross the river, but ten-year-old Suntae who couldn't see didn't know the way. He had to try to remember the way he had gone before to get to his aunt's house in Yangju, absolutely not an easy task.

Suntae started to sing a hymn from Sunday school.

Jesus loves me! This I know,
For the Bible tells me so.
Little ones to Him belong;
They are weak, but He is strong

Suntae couldn't get his bearings or sense of direction, but after he crossed the river he started to find the way by listening. He tried not to miss the sound of fleeing people's footsteps and carts. When he heard farmers working in the nearby fields, he begged, "Please, give me some food. Give me some food." During war time, food was precious to everyone. Some farmers were kind enough to share the lunch they had carried into the fields with Suntae. They willingly gave him the rice and radish kimchi that was left in their lunch gourd. Even with this humble food, Suntae was so hungry it felt like he was eating heavenly food.

Suntae thought, 'A Long time ago when the Hebrews were traveling with Moses, God sent them manna from heaven. Manna must have tasted the same as this food.'

> *The people of Israel called the bread manna. It was white like coriander seed and tasted like wafers made with honey.*
>
> **Exodus 16:31**

> *The Israelites ate manna forty years, until they came to a land that was settled; they ate manna until they reached the border of Canaan.*
>
> **Exodus 16:35**

Thanks to all the warm-hearted people, Suntae was able to survive without starving on his dangerous wartime trip to Yangju. Suntae crossed rivers, mountains and streams. He even tripped and fell down because of the ditches in the rice-fields, rolling over and over. Fallen and bruised by this way of traveling, he just kept traveling to his aunt's house. The poor blind boy only thought about surviving his trip by relying on his strong faith and words from the Bible.

> *But now, this is what the Lord says — he who created you, Jacob, he who formed you, Israel: "Do not fear, for I have redeemed you; I have summoned you by name; you are mine. When you pass through the waters, I will be with you; and when you pass through the rivers, they will not sweep over you. When you walk through the fire, you will not be burned; the flames will not set you ablaze. For I am the Lord your God, the Holy One of Israel, your Savior; I give Egypt for your ransom, Cush and Seba in your stead.*
>
> **Isaiah 43:1-3**

At last, Suntae finally arrived at his aunt's house! Suntae felt great relief of joy. He could actually feel hope and happiness falling on his shoulders like snowflakes. Finally, Suntae was safe.

When he arrived, he called, "Aunt" with great joy in front of her house. He yelled louder, "Aunt! Aunt!"

"Who's there?"

Suntae finally got to meet his aunt again.

His aunt was surprised to see Suntae. She asked, "What are you doing here? And why are you so dirty like a beggar?"

Probably, his aunt remembered Suntae as the precious only son of his family who was lavished with love and attention by his parents and grandmother. Suntae told her what happened back in Seoul when his house was bombed. He told her in detail the shocking stories of how he lost his parents, house and eyesight. Suntae expected his aunt to hug her nephew and comfort him for his tragedy. He needed encouragement and a warm welcome from his aunt. However, after Suntae finished his story his aunt responded coldly,

"Blind people are useless in this world. Cows need eyes to work and dogs also need eyes to keep houses safe. But you are blind so you have no need or reason to be allowed to live in this world. Leave my house and never come back. I don't care if you drown in the river, get beaten up, or get shot. If a home has a blind person like you in it it won't have any luck, and you will bring shame and criticism to us. Others will view our household as cursed, so leave us quickly!"

His aunt gave a feeble excuse that since she lived with her parents-in-law the house was too crowded for Suntae to stay. Suntae was shocked and speechless. He had gone through all kinds of difficulties to meet the only relative he had left, but she did not welcome him at all. Instead she wished him to dead and buried. Suntae had strongly believed that when he met his aunt she would help him go back to school and get eye treatment like his own parents would have. He had gambled his life in the hope of meeting his aunt. He could not believe the horrible things he just heard from his aunt. Although Suntae was indescribably heartbroken, he wanted to believe his aunt reacted that way because she was also shocked. He decided he would stay at her house for a while. However, his aunt didn't change at all even after time passed. While staying at her house, Suntae experienced a living-hell that he wouldn't forget for the rest of his life Suntae's only hope was crushed. He had firmly believed that the only hope for him now was with his aunt, without doubt the only one who could save him he had thought. But all those dreams had fallen apart.

Chapter 4

Painful
Memories

Suntae's aunt's family was wealthy enough to have a large farmland and a couple of cows with some servants working for them. In the evening, his aunt's family and neighbors had a great time together, making a fire and roasting corn and potatoes.

However, this pleasure was not allowed to Suntae. From morning till night, his aunt abused him verbally. "You should die! Get out of my house!" She cursed him so severely all the time. Even worse, she beat him day in and day out. His daily beatings left Suntae with black and blue bruises all over his body.

Not a single day passed without his being battered by the aunt's family members. One time they hit him with a dried tree branch. His flesh was torn off by the thorns of the branches. Suntae rolled on the floor in great pain and begged them to stop.

One day, he was hit with an iron poker. He was hurt so badly that blood ran down from his head, but he had no one to treat his wound. Suntae was deeply traumatized, physically and mentally, by his hurts and sorrow.

One morning, all the other people went out to work leaving only Suntae, his aunt, and the grandmother at the house. His aunt took him to a room and closed the door. Then, she began beating him up with a hayfork and scratching his face with her fingernails. Because Suntae got beaten up so brutally, he threw up all the food he had eaten the day before. At that moment, one woman in his neighborhood came by to borrow something and saw the scene.

"Why are you hitting this poor child?" she asked the aunt anxiously. "He behaved badly so I am teaching him a lesson," his aunt lied in reply. Out of pity, the woman brought Suntae a cup of cold water from the well and kindly wiped the wounds and scratches on his face with her saliva to treat the skin. "I want to put some medicine on your face, but I have nothing right now. In my experience, saliva works well for wounds, too," she said. Maybe that saliva didn't work on Suntae. His face itched badly to the point that he couldn't stand it. He rubbed and washed his face for several days. Then the scars started to disappear, but he was left with two warts under the eyes.

One sizzling summer day in August, 1950, his aunt gave him a bowl of brown rice and chilled cucumber soup. Suntae thought for a moment, 'What is with her today? Why is she so nice to me?' but he gobbled up everything. Then, the grandmother ordered him, "Follow me. Go to the garden and carry back as many pumpkins as you can."

Suntae was only a 10-year-old skinny boy since he hadn't had a decent meal or enough sleep for several months. Of course carrying a heavy a-frame on his back when they told him to do so was too much for this little boy. Although he managed to put it on his shoulders, the carrier was too big for his body, so he just dragged it along. He couldn't even walk out the gate with it on. One of aunt's servants shortened the shoulder straps of the carrier to help him walk more freely. Suntae and the grandmother crossed a stream and walked across the garden patch to their farmland. After a long walk, they arrived at the garden. Yellow melons as well as pumpkins were picked and packed in boxes to be sold. The sweet scent of melons reminded him of the time he used to swim and eat chilled melon with his old friends. His mouth watered as he was famished, but nobody offered him a slice.

Evening came and Suntae tried to stand up with an a-frame full of pumpkins on his shoulders. He fell to the ground, with the carrier and all the pumpkins and melons all spilled out. "Do you have any idea how much all these cost? You're nothing but a worthless blind boy," yelled grandmother. Grandfather and his uncles, who were picking up pumpkins together, said "Let's kick Suntae out! He is utterly useless!" and dragged him off somewhere.

"Here is where you must live from now on!"

All of a sudden, he was alone in strange place, much like a barn.

'Where am I? Is this place empty? Who is living here? How far am I from aunt's house?' He had so many questions but there was no one to answer him. He desperately kept feeling around the room but he could only feel some strange objects.

Throughout the night, he heard a cat's cry and thought that sound might be from a fox or wolf nearby. Being alone in this strange place, he became terrified. He kept feeling around and managed to get outside. There was a large tree. He climbed up in the tree to save himself from wild foxes or wolves. He spent the whole night in the tree, shivering with fright.

At last, sunlight hit his eyes. Soon, he heard people going to work. The sound of a cowbell drew near to him. "Mister, please help me. Please tell me where I am!" said Suntae. The surprised farmer answered, "Where did you come from? You are at the house for dead corpses." Suntae felt a chill running down his spine with a horror that was different from what he had felt the night before.

The kind farmer helped Suntae down from the tree and brought him to the field. He even offered some of the food he had brought for lunch. Then the kind farmer led Suntae back to his aunt's house.

As soon as his aunt saw Suntae again, she yelled with disappointment, "Why did you come back? I wished a devil would take you away. Now all our neighbors know our family's shame, which is you! I can't live with this shame!" Grandmother took him to the storage room and beat him again. Everything at his aunt's house turned out to be the opposite of what he had expected. Everything only got worse day by day. Everybody in the family wished Suntae would go away as soon as possible. Maybe they thought he would leave on his own if they treated him badly.

This hymn clearly describes what Suntae went through back then.

Nobody knows the trouble I've seen—Nobody knows but Jesus
Nobody knows the trouble I've seen—Glory hallelujah!
Sometimes I'm up, sometimes I'm down—Oh, yes, Lord
Sometimes I'm almost to the ground—Oh, yes, Lord
Although you see me going 'long so—Oh, yes, Lord
I have my trials here below—Oh, yes, Lord
If you get there before I do—Oh, yes, Lord
Tell all-a my friends I'm coming too—Oh, yes, Lord

Chapter 5

Death's Doorstep

As the Korean War became prolonged, North Korean troops broke into any house they saw. After stealing valuables in the house, theywould kill people and set fire to the house. Yet during those times of war, Koreans still celebrated the Harvest Day, Chusok, in September. All the family at aunt's gathered around and ate *pindae ddok* bean pancake and chicken to celebrate the Harvest Day.

His aunt ordered Suntae to stay in the backyard and not let even the sound of his breathing be heard, far from the relatives until they were all gone. His Aunt was scary. Suntae was sure he would be beaten by her if he would show up, so he stayed quiet until everybody left. 'If I hide here quietly all day, my aunt will think that I'm a good boy,' he thought. 'When will aunt call me in, talk nice because I was quiet and give me all the delicious food?' He couldn't wait.

At last, grandmother called out to Suntae from the backyard and he hoped that now he would get some of the holiday food, but she said, "Go to the mountain and cut an a-frame full of grass to feed the ox. Unless you do that, there will be no dinner for you!" His mind went blank because it was impossible for the hungry boy to climb up the mountain, cut grass, and carry it back down to home. Not to mention

Suntae's disappointment that there would be no holiday food left for him. Even worse, the mountain was known to be dangerous with its cliffs and snakes. However, there was no other option for Suntae.

Finally, Suntae headed to the mountain with an a-frame on his back. He had never used a sickle before. He tried to cut grass, only to hurt his second finger. He had to wait for a while until the blood stopped after he wrapped the wounded finger with leaves. Sitting alone in the dark, he thought that he must look depressingly pathetic. There was no hope in sight. "Killing myself would be much better than living like this." He firmly decided to kill himself and began strangling himself with his belt.

At that moment, he heard a mysterious voice out of the air.

"Stop it! The day will come when you will grow up and tell your story of these events."

Out of surprise, he stopped strangling himself and turned around. He could not sense anyone around but still the strange voice kept echoing in his ears.

After a while, the grandmother and a cousin came to the mountain to find him. Grandmother beat him up again with a stick after she found out that Suntae didn't bring any grass back home. "Help me, please, help me!" No matter how loudly he shouted, there was no one on the mountain around him to help.

Suntae came home, with his arms and legs swollen from all the beating. His aunt put a bowl of rice and water in front of him for supper. Then, his aunt and the grandmother sat beside him and cursed him saying, "As you eat that, choke on it an die!" They took turns smacking him hard. Suntae was so famished that he ignored them and kept eating his food. The very fact that he was eating while enduring all this humiliation made Suntae despise himself. He made himself a promise to put his suicidal thoughts into practice that very night.

Late at night, while everyone was sleeping, he crawled into the well headlong. His life was a living-hell. He was just an inch away from putting his nose and mouth into the water. Soon he would be dead.

Then came the voice again.

"Stop everything. Get out of the well right now. I will guide your way."

It was as if someone was pulling his feet out of the well. Suntae's second suicide attempt failed again.

On September 28th, 1950 the South reclaimed Seoul from the North. Many people thought that the northern forces had withdrawn for good and that they could finally live peacefully without any trouble. To put all the tragedy behind, people performed spiritual rituals to expel evil spirits. In Korea, rice cakes and seven bowls of rice should be served during the ritual. These rice bowls are called "meals for the dead." People should not eat these making sure to throw the rice away no matter what. People believed that eating it would curse them to die, get sick, or have a poor harvest that fall.

His aunt's house was no exception. They hired two shamans, prepared the traditional offerings of rice cakes and boiled rice, and performed the ritual for several days. At that night, aunt brought a full bowl of rice for Suntae. Since a handful of rice with kimchi was the usual meal for Suntae, he thought 'Today is special.' Not suspecting anything, Suntae happily ate up all his meal feeling lucky.

Several days later, a servant at aunt's house told him shocking news.

"Didn't you eat a large meal the other day? Do you want to know what you really ate? You ate the meal for dead people. We wished you would die after eating it. Seeing that nothing happened to you, I'm quite sure you will live a long life. Even ghosts cannot take your life away."

His aunt's family believed in Buddhism and superstitions. They might be afraid that having a blind kid in the home would curse the whole family.

Summer and fall came to an end and it was now winter with its cold winds. That made Suntae's life even more miserable. Staying at his aunt's house in summer was bad enough, but winter was even harder to bear. He was not allowed to sleep inside the heated rooms of the house, instead he slept on the rice bag on the wooden floor outside. When it was freezing cold, he slept with his two feet in the fire hole outside a heated room. There were two friendly dogs at aunt's house. They kept him warm and became good friends of Suntae which helped to ease his loneliness and fear.

One December day, the harvest was over and people had to go south to take refuge again. People wrapped their things to take in bundles that had to be loaded on the backs of people or a horse or cow. His aunt's family also decided to flee from the war and plotted a terrible, cruel plan the day before they were to leave the town.

"Suntae will be nothing but a burden on our way. We cannot bring him with us nor leave him behind in this house. So let's feed him a breakfast mixed with poison. This time he will be dead for good. Then we can leave this town after we bury him on the mountain."

He happened to overhear this conversation. He shivered out of panic, shaking like a leaf. With no one to depend on and no place where he could run away to, Suntae was completely terrified, thinking 'Am I really supposed to die tomorrow morning after eating poisoned rice?'

At that moment, what he had heard from the pastor came to his mind. 'Come what may, if you pray to the living God, he will listen to you.' So he whispered a short, desperate prayer to God.

"God, am I supposed to die eating poisoned rice tomorrow morning?"

Then he thought he heard what must have been God's voice.

"Suntae, rise up and leave this place!"

Suntae prayed and prayed. With each prayer, Suntae heard the voice of the Lord telling him to leave the town.

The Lord had said to Abram, 'Go from your country, your people and your father's household to the land I will show you. I will make you into a great nation, and I will bless you; I will make your name great, and you will be a blessing. I will bless those who bless you, and whoever curses you I will curse; and all peoples on earth will be blessed through you.' **Genesis 12:1-3**

Chapter 6

Run for
Your Life!

Suntae continuously heard God's voice inside him. He finally made up his mind to run away. That night, he quietly opened the front door and sneaked out of the house when his aunt and the others were all asleep. He did not say goodbye to anyone as he ran away. Only the two puppies, Goldie and Whitey, followed behind him.

Suntae said, "Farewell Goldie and Whitey. Go inside now. I must run far away." However, the puppies accompanied him for several miles.

"I am not sure when I will see you again. I have to go far away, but I will always miss you."

He did not say goodbye to anyone as he ran away. Only the two puppies, Goldie and Whitey, followed walking behind him.

"I am not sure when I will see you again. I will always miss you."

Suntae patted the puppies on their heads with his hand which was wet from wiping his tears. Although they were animals he felt thankful that they followed him to see him off.

Suntae's long painful journey had started. After saying farewell to the puppies he went traveling the mountain road wearing only thin straw shoes in the cold winter weather. Blind Suntae could not let his guard down even just for one second as the mountain was full of icy streams and bumpy fields.

Finally, when he reached the main road he felt relieved and wanted to shout out loudly, 'I am saved.'

The young boy got courage remembering one of the pastor's sermons about how Moses escaped from Egypt with the Hebrew people. They ran away for their lives in the middle of the night relying only on God's word.

The night of December 22ⁿᵈ, 1950 was a victorious day for Suntae to overcome his doubts about escaping and feeling lost. His thoughts of death were transformed into bravery and hope.At that time, actually it was thought to be the most challenging day for Suntae even more challenging than the day when he crossed the Han River to go to his aunt's house thinking it was his only hope.

Suntae was scared that his aunt's family might catch him so he had to run away as far as he could, swept along by crowds of refugees moving in lines of people fleeing to the South. What he experienced then was similar to the Israelites' exodus and escape from the Egyptian soldiers. Suntae promised himself that he would never go back to his aunt's house again.

Suntae realized that from now on God was the only savior whom he could trust.

"Father, if you let me live I promise that I will be successful one day. I will dedicate my life to people like me who cannot see."

Suntae's prayer was desperate. He tried to overcome his fear by singing hymns he learned at Sunday school.

Jesus is our bright light
He says to us as He shines,

'You are the light of the world,
You are the light of the world!'

Suntae ran as fast as he could. His body felt frozen but strangely his back, hands and feet felt warm. Perhaps God was his shepherd holding Suntae's body tightly in His arms.

Have I not commended you? Be strong and courageous. Do not be
afraid; do not be discouraged, for the Lord your God will be with you
wherever you go. **Joshua 1:9**

One winter day when the wind was so cold it cut through one's skin like a knife, Suntae lagged behind other refugees in a remote valley in North Kyungsang Province. An old man he met by chance told him that there was a town not far from there. Although Suntae had to go through a deep valley, he continued his journey on the dangerous road to find the town. He only had a small wooden stick in his hand to find his way as he crossed a frozen stream. Suntae had no clue about how far away the town was and even if he arrived at the town he didn't know anyone so he would have no place to stay. His heart felt frozen and paralyzed by the thought of going to a place where no one was waiting for him.

Suntae heard faint sound of a dog barking faraway.

"I must be near the town. Let's try whistling."

Suntae whistled to dogs over and over to check if the town was close to him. As he got closer to a town the dogs barked back louder. At last, when Suntae heard loud barking from different directions, he knew clearly that he was near the town.

'I have survived!'

Suntae ended up standing in front of a house. He pushed the gate open carefully and went to the house. He called, "Is anyone here? Please help me."

There was no sound of a person in the house.

People had become indifferent since the war broke out—everyday so many people cried for help in the street.

However, Suntae did not give up and shouted even louder, "Please help me!"

A few minutes later, someone came out and saw a little blind boy. He took the boy into his hut and made him a straw bed. The straw bed was not as warm as a heated floor room, however, in winter it served as a comfortable shelter from the biting wind if one stayed deep under the straw.

Not many people were kind enough to let a beggar stay at their house over night. In fact, Suntae looked like a beggar and refugee after his long tiring journey. Suntae felt very thankful towards the man who provided him a place in the hut and a straw bed. Usually people kicked him out for simply seeking shelter from the rain under their overhanging roof.

Truly I tell you, anyone who gives you a cup of water in my name because you belong to the Messiah will certainly not lose their reward.

Mark 9:41

Suntae's trip after he escaped cannot be described in any way as comfortable or happy, but rather as the life of a lonely and miserable beggar boy. At least he was safe from the rain when he was with his aunt, but after the escape every day was a battle to find food and shelter. Nevertheless, Suntae promised himself that he would survive. Now he had no plans to die. Rather, he had a new hope to sacrifice himself so that later he would be able to help other visually disabled people.

Suntae never skipped Sunday school even though his parents and grandmother, who had a strong faith in Buddhism, always forbade him from going. Whenever difficult things happened to him he prayed that the Lord would lead him and remembered the words of his pastor and the Bible. Slowly Suntae was changing into a boy with strong faith and hope in the midst of pain.

Later, Suntae read the following verses and realized that following the word of God had led his way.

In my distress I called to the Lord; I cried to my God for help. From his temple he heard my voice; my cry came before him, into his ears.
Psalm 118:6

The Lord is with me; I will not be afraid. What can mere mortals do to me?
Psalm 118:6

Part 2
Racing to the End of Darkness

Chapter 7

The Only Thing
a Blind Boy Can Do

Suntae spent two years wandering around all over Korea through six provinces as a beggar: Icheon, Yeoju, Ansung, Chungchung, Umsung, Jincheon, Daejeon, Daegu, Youngju, Andong, Jeonla and Busan were the names of cities and towns he visited.

If you pick the best season for beggars, it would be summer. You can stay anywhere because of the weather with its nice warm breezes. The only bad part is being caught in the rain, but that's not all bad. You can take a refreshing shower in the rain which beggars need because they can't bathe like most people.

Winter is the most horrible season for beggars. You always have to worry about where to spend the night. You have to escape the cold wind by huddling under a roof or the front of houses. When morning comes, you have to stretch and shake your body to warm up because if you don't move your body for a long time, you will freeze to death.

Suntae crossed dangerous rivers and walked through the mountains. Whenever he got scared, perhaps because of hearing the sound of wild animals, he sang the hymns he had learned at Sunday school to overcome his fear.

Leaning, leaning, safe and
secure from all alarms;
Leaning, Leaning, leaning
on the everlasting arms.
What have I to dread, what have I fear,
leaning on the everlasting arms.
I have blessed peace with my Lord so near,
leaning on the everlasting arms.

In those days, you could easily see beggars in Busan station or in large markets throughout Busan, or else beggars going from inn to inn or house to house begging. There were many beggars who joined together and they had their own beggar way of life with a strict set of rules. Each beggar gang was assigned their own territory to beg in. One who broke into another's territory ended up being beaten, or even being killed. That was the rule for beggars and street gangs. It was not an easy life but all about tough competition for survival. Suntae decided to go back to his hometown, Seoul. During that time, many US troops were stationed in the Seoul area and they were very generous to poor children. Hearing about this, Suntae decided that life in Seoul would be better than life in Busan.

Now, the biggest problem was finding a way to get Seoul. Suntae had to get on a train to Seoul, but he didn't have money for a ticket. So he had no choice but to sneak into a slow train going to Seoul. When a conductor came to ask for his ticket, he hid under the seats. Sometimes kind passengers next to him helped him to hide in the bathroom.

Finally, as the stow away Suntae approached the city of Seoul, he realized he had another problem. Seoul was at war so you needed to show a pass to cross the Han River. Unfortunately, without that pass he had no other choice but to get off the train at Youngdeungpo Station, one station before the Han River.

Now Suntae was about to start his life over again as a beggar in Seoul. He was already used to begging, so surely he could get along from day to day. However, this way of life was hopeless and miserable with no end in sight.

Then one day, as Suntae was crossing the Han River, he ran into a US soldier guarding the bridge. 'Hello', 'Help me', 'Please give me', and 'Thank you' were all he could say in English, but Suntae bravely approached the soldier. He said to the soldier, "Please, help me!"

The soldier felt sympathy for the blind and scared little beggar in front him so he took Suntae to his headquarters. The soldier allowed Suntae to warm himself, made him a cup of hot cocoa, and gave him socks and underwear.

"Thank you. Thank you. Thank you so much." Speaking in English and Korean Suntae bowed to the soldier more than ten times because it meant so much to him.

The soldier's benevolence didn't end there. He contacted different places and finally sent him to the Italian hospital which was set up in Usin Elementary School in Yeongdeungpo. Suntae hadn't enjoyed this kind of warm comfort for a long time. For two months there, he received treatment for his sores. He learned how to say 'good morning' in Italian, "Buon Giorno!"

For the first time, Suntae was not concerned about having to get food every day. His life in the hospital reminded him of the heaven he learned of in Sunday school and he thought, 'If heaven really exists, then this must be heaven.'

After his treatment was all finished, the US soldier took him to Sam Ae Orphanage, located at the foot of Namsan Mountain in Seoul. Suntae repeatedly thanked the soldier for his kindness.

Sun Ae Orphanage was home for over 300 orphaned children, providing three meals a day and clean shelter. He still suffered because he was the only blind boy in the orphanage.

The other orphans bullied him. What made him more miserable was the fact that everyone except Suntae had chance to study at school. Suntae's existence was nothing more than remaining a victim of bullying and beatings when everyone else was getting a proper education at school.

Several times he desperately asked the director of the orphanage to let him study. Sadly, the chief always rejected the request by saying that it is impossible for a blind child to study with other students who were not disabled. Suntae could not accept the fact and did not want to live without thinking of the future so he made up his mind. After just a month since arriving at Sun Ae Orphanage, he left saying goodbye to the orphanage director.

Suntae's strong desire to study made him leave the orphanage, however, he did not know what to do next. Although everything seemed elusive and impossible, he started his new journey just like the time when he left his aunt's house. He looked neat and tidy with the clean clothes he had gotten from the US soldier. So people no longer gave money to him. Older street kids took away Suntae's new clothes and left him with their old dirty ones. Now Suntae looked exactly like the beggar he had been a few months before. He started begging again, wandering through Seoul Station and the markets.

He was nothing more than a street kid in the chaos of the Korean War, but there was always the idea in Suntae's heart that he was the son of a king. Suntae was a dear son of God, and he always found a ray of hope within God's grace.

> *Not only so, but we also glory in our sufferings, because we know that suffering produces perseverance; perseverance, character; and character, hope.*   **Romans 5:3-4**

Chapter 8

The Trials of the Orphanage

Blind Suntae was walking around the street holding his food can in his hand. Suddenly a stranger grabbed his arm.

The stranger turned out to be an American army chaplain. The kind chaplain brought Suntae to his home and let him take a shower and change into new clothes. Then the pastor took the poor boy to the Amazing Love Orphanage of 400 to 500 children run by a Methodist pastor in Yongsan. The chaplain came to visit once every two weeks giving the children chocolate, cookies and bread. Also he was kind enough to teach them English words whenever he visited.

Suntae still slept on a cold floor. His room was freezing since the orphanage rooms were heated by stoves which only provided a feeble amount of heat for the twenty or thirty children sleeping nearest to the stove.

At night, when the children who were sleeping upstairs urinated, it leaked down onto those downstairs. Sometimes urine dripped onto those sleeping below even into their faces and mouths. In fact, there was no real ceiling and only a layer of planks made up the upstairs floor so the children sleeping downstairs sometimes got a shower of urine.

The food was awful compared to the Sam Ae Orphanage. They only served two meals a day. The only food the children to eat was brown rice mixed with salt given by the American military.

The orphans in this facility were divided into three main groups: the children working in the vegetable plots around the orphanage, others going to school and children six years of age and under.

Suntae did not fit into any one of these groups. Even worse, the children always laughed at his different way of acting as if he were a monkey. The older kids brutally beat Suntae, kicking him and hitting his face with their fists. Wherever Suntae stayed, living with children who were not disabled always turned out to be painful for him. By the time Suntae started to think this place was not for him, somebody whispered in his ear secretly.

"There is an orphanage for disabled children near Yongsan, called the Horizon Orphanage. They provide education for disabled children appropriate for each individual's disability."

When Suntae heard the news, he was excited and filled with hope. Immediately, Suntae went to the unordained pastor in charge and asked to be transferred to the Horizon Orphanage. A teacher took Suntae to the new orphanage, 30-40 minutes away from where he had been staying.

Those in the Horizon Orphanage were of different ages from children to adults with a wide range of disabilities.

A total of 200 people were living together including people with epilepsy, those with mental disabilities and those who had lost legs or had other physical disabilities. Among them, there were about 10 people with visual impairment including Suntae. The Horizon Orphanage was full of unfortunate people, some with severe multiple disabilities. It was common for the epileptics to have seizures causing them to fall down and froth at the mouth. Even worse, there were some who ate their own feces, or others who ran about threatening to kill those around them with scissors. The Horizon Orphanage only provided meals twice a day. Sometimes the stronger orphas took away the weaker disabled ones' food by force, so unfortunately the hungry weaker orphans had to go out on the street desperately begging for something to eat.

Once in a while, teachers would beat up the students for no reason. Also, the school janitor sometimes battered the students with brooms when he was having a bad day.

Whenever this happened, Suntae wanted to leave this place for which he had no love because of the violence and cruel treatment toward the disabled. Meanwhile, there was a girl a few years older than Suntae, named Euijin, whose right foot had been cut off during the bombing. She took good care of Suntae. Now and then she would offer him some jelly and bread, as well as, some good advice.

"Suntae, don't even think about running away to become a beggar. It would be difficult, but there are schools for those blind like you where you can get a good education. You must have hope and find a school like that. You are smart and handsome, so study hard to become a great person."

Thus, Suntae found out that there actually were schools for the blind.

Although Suntae had difficult time enduring orphanage life, at the same time, he also learned some valuable lessons. There were many times when Suntae wished to die. He found out that he couldn't study with normal children. However, he found out in the orphanages that there were so many other war orphans whose situations were worse than his. So Suntae came to realize that he was too healthy in body and spirit to live being negative and pessimistic about the world.

Suntae's body was shivering with cold and all over his body he was covered with wounds and bruises, yet he had no one to rely on in this world. All during this difficult time, he could hear God encouraging him with love and endurance. "Hold on. Suntae, hold on to Me," said God.

> *When hard pressed, I cried to the Lord; he brought me into a spacious place. The Lord is with me; I will not be afraid. What can mere mortals do to me? The Lord is with me; he is my helper. I look in triumph on my enemies.* **Psalm 118:5-7**

Suntae became good friends with a boy named Jung-Woon Kim at the Horizon Orphanage. Jung-Woon's right leg was crippled from a festering wound. Jung-Woon was like a brother to Suntae in the way they helped one another.

One day, the two friends promised each other to run away together. They both were sure if they stayed there they would end up crazy with even more severe disabilities.

"Where should we go?"

"Let's go to Chuncheon."

"Chuncheon?"

"Yes. There are many American soldiers, so we will be able to make a living by begging. American soldiers are very generous to orphans like us. Let's go there."

"Okay. First, we must run away from Seoul as soon as possible."

Suntae and Jung-Woon had to leave Seoul quickly, because if they got caught they would be beaten to death.

After breakfast, Suntae and Jung-Woon escaped from the Horizon Orphanage going down a side alley to Samgak Intersection. Luckily, just then there was an American military truck going to Chuncheon. Feeling lucky, the two boys sneaked into the truck.

Right before they arrived in Chuncheon, the truck was inspected by the guards. However, Suntae and Jung-Woon, of course, did not have any form of I.D. That day, the weather was extremely cold, so the American soldier in the truck took the boys to a tent to get warm and let them drink hot cocoa. Then the soldier took them back to Seoul in the truck. When they arrived in Seoul, the kind soldier gave them some food and a couple of dollars. Suntae and Jung-Woon couldn't stay in Seoul and had no time to waste. They ran to the Yongsan station and got on a train to Busan.

In Busan, there was nobody waiting for the poor boys. The blind orphan's journey continued like that, with only his crippled friend by his side.

Suntae still clearly remembers the following verse from Psalms, which he memorized while he lived as an orphan.

I lift up my eyes to the mountains—where does my help come from? My help comes from the Lord, the Maker of heaven and earth. He will not let your foot slip—he who watches over you will not slumber; indeed, he who watches over Israel will neither slumber nor sleep. The Lord watches over you — the Lord is your shade at your right hand; the sun will not harm you by day, nor the moon by night.

The Lord will keep you from all harm — he will watch over your life; the Lord will watch over your coming and going both now and forevermore. **Psalm 121**

Chapter 9

The Way to Become King of Beggars

During the bitter cold winter days, beggars' lives become even more painful and miserable. Where to spend the night is their biggest concern.

The luckiest day for a beggar is to find a warm fire hole at someone's house. However, not all beggars can have this kind of comfortable night. Only the leader of the beggars, the most powerful and experienced one, can have this luxury. It is unimaginable for rookies to spend a night in a warm place.

Suntae thought, 'How can I become the leader and get the warm place beside the fire hole?'

This was a matter of life and death because if he fell asleep on the cold street, he could freeze to death.

The fastest way to rise to the leader position was quite simple – sharing food with the other beggars, instead of keeping all the food for oneself. Of course, it was not easy to share food with others. As a street beggar, the food one got from begging was all he had. Accordingly, giving food to others was almost equal to giving his entire fortune to someone else.

Suntae was smart enough to know the trick to leadership. Suntae knew that once he generously gave everything to the younger rookie beggars, they would willingly look after him. After Suntae tirelessly begged for money, rice, cookies and bread, day or night he generously gave out the food to other beggars gathered under a straw roof or in a sunny place. Several days had passed and the younger beggars began to follow him. Now Suntae rose up to the top of the beggar hierarchy. Although, some beggars were older and stronger than he was, when he also gave them the food that he gotten by begging as well as using money he had received to buy candy and bread for them. They were so touched by Suntae's benevolence that they started to protect Suntae.

"If anyone treats Suntae badly, they will have to answer to us." As the news of what the stronger beggars were saying spread through the beggar society, even more beggars wanted to be Suntae's followers and about ten rookie beggars became devoted followers. Suntae won the respect from his beggars as their benevolent leader.

This taught him a big lesson. Sharing with others is always the best way to overcome all the obstacles. Suntae expanded his influence becoming leader of all the beggars in the area from the train station to the fish market. Early in the morning, each beggar started their day with an empty can, begging from door to door. Most beggars failed to get food from time to time. However, Suntae was exceptional as the ladies working at restaurants always gave Suntae a full can of food.

"Suntae. We haven't even opened the restaurant yet, but here is some food for you. Eat until you are full and grow up to become a good person."

"Your nose is cute looking. It tells me that you will be blessed in the future." Some people even gave words of support and consolation to him.

Every evening, finding a place to spend the night was the most difficult task of the day. However, now that Suntae was the leader of the beggars, he could sleep in the best place under the rules of the beggar society. Suntae came to the realization that living for others gives joy to the Father in heaven and brings respect and recognition from others. Suntae through his society of beggars learned the wisdom and mercy of sharing with other people.

Suppose a brother or sister is without clothes and daily food. If one of you says to him, "Go, I wish you well; keep warm and well fed," but does nothing about his physical needs, what good is it? In the same way, faith by itself, if it is not accompanied by action, is dead.

James 2:15-17

Four things are required to win respect from other beggars. First, a large empty can, a necessary tool for a beggar, Second, stubbornness, Third, courage and Fourth, patience.

On top of these four things, Suntae was armed with an additional two virtues, love and sympathy. Given these traits, it was no coincidence that Suntae maintained his leadership for a long time. In fact, there was another virtue that he kept to himself; no matter what happened, going to church without fail every Sunday.

Sometimes thinking a beggar whose clothes are full of patches has come, a church wouldn't let him come in. Another day, a church might gave him some money and kick him out. Amid such humiliation, Suntae thought that they only misunderstood him and he went to another church without complaining, still believing that he was also a cherished son of the King in the kingdom of heaven.

Sometimes, he got skin rashes and looked like a leper, but he headed toward church determined to celebrate Sunday and worship God, so he looked here and there for a place he could worship. When a church didn't let him enter, or even worse, when its members lashed out with humiliating words, although he could not worship there, without harsh feelings he said a tearful prayer for them.

"Although I'm just a filthy beggar in other people's eye, I hope someday, to live up to my potential as God's child. Please bestow on me a strong courage so that I can endure all this humiliation until that day." On days when he could not enter a church, a tearful Suntae prayed even more earnestly.

"Please give me enough love to forgive others just as Jesus gave up his life to forgive us. Please change them into people of strong faith who know the love of the Father." He prayed this way to God for the people who threw stones and spit on him, calling him a leper.

And Suntae decided to spread the gospel of Jesus to those who didn't know the Lord. To that end, the first thing he did was to encourage his followers to go to church whenever they came back with no food. Usually, beggars were expected to be beaten up by their leader if they couldn't get any food. Even worse, some beggars were battered badly to the point of losing consciousness. Surprisingly, Suntae said to the younger beggars when they came back empty-handed, "If you go to church with me, I will use my money and buy you tasty treats." He bought delicious bread for the beggars who memorized what was taught in Sunday School: "For God so loved the world that he gave his one and only Son, that whoever believes in him shall not perish but have eternal life (John

3:16)."

That's how Suntae was able to take the rookie beggars with him to church every week. At church, he donated the cleanest cash he had collected. He never missed a single Sunday in going to church.

Remember the Sabbath day by keeping it holy.

Exodus 20:8

But showing love to a thousand generations of those who love me and keep my commandments.

Deuteronomy 5:10

Chapter 10

The Compassion
of a Stranger

One night Suntae was looking for a place to stay overnight in a small town. There was one house with stacks of firewood in the storage area. Suntae quietly stole into the yard and spent a night in the little hut. Unfortunately, the next day his whole body from head to toe started to itch and later he broke out in a rash all over his skin.

"What is happening to me? Was I bitten by a flea, a mouse, or a louse?"

Suntae ignored the rash for a few days hoping they would get better naturally. However, as time passed, his skin stung even worse and yellow liquid started oozing out from the sores. He felt like his whole body was festering. When Suntae begged for food from house to house, people splashed him with water or threw rocks at him, thinking he was a leper. Some cold-hearted people even released their hungry dogs to attack him and chase him away.

Later Suntae couldn't even move one step further because his stomach ached so much. Poison from his skin must have infected his stomach too. Also he lost his voice. The worst part was that because his skin was so swollen with this stinking pus liquid, whenever he touched his face with fingers, yellow pus would ooze out and his skin sank in, like soft bread dough. His pain was only getting worse every day. Several days later, Suntae was begging around the town with so much pain in his body. He suddenly felt he was the unluckiest person in the world. He could not control his emotion. He sat under the tree clutching his beggar's can and started to weep sorrowfully. God must have heard Suntae's painful cry. That moment, an old lady passed by him singing a hymn.

> *I know not why God's wondrous grace*
> *To me He hath made known,*
> *Nor why, unworthy, Christ in love*
> *Redeemed me for His own.*
> *I know not how this saving faith*
> *To me He did impart,*
> *Nor how believing in His word*
> *Wrought peace within my heart.*

The old lady singing the hymn stopped in front of Suntae and said,

"Little boy. You seem like you are infected by lacquer poison. The poison must have gone deep into your body, what can we do? Let me see your hand."

Suntae explained his situation tearfully, reaching out his filthy hand to the lady. Surprisingly, she held his hand tightly and prayed for him.

"Dear God. Please heal this poor boy's poisoned skin."

After prying the lady tried to comfort him.

"Don't be discouraged. Even though you would feel that the world abandoned you, Jesus always loves you. God will guide your way."

God, who loves Suntae, speaks this way in the Bible.

"Because he loves me," says the Lord, "I will rescue him; I will protect him, for he acknowledges my name. He will call on me, and I will answer him; I will be with him in trouble, I will deliver him and honor him. With long life I will satisfy him and show him my salvation." **Psalm 91:14–16**

The kind lady went on her way leaving behind Suntae all alone. Strangely he could feel a small hope inside of him encouraging him to think only about the bright future that lay ahead of him. Her kindness opened up his heart and healed his wounds.

Suntae sat down under the tree for couple of more hours. He did not have the strenght to stand up so he just sat there staring at the sky. Then he heard the footsteps of the old lady coming back towards him.

"I was worried you wouldn't be here. Let's go to my house. I could not stop thinking about you. You must be an angel sent by God."

The kind lady held Suntae's hand and took him to her place. She took off all his dirty clothes and gave him a nice warm bath. Then after praying to God, she sucked and spit out all the poisonous liquid from his infected skin.

For the next 20 days, she took good care of Suntae with love and affection. Thanks to her warm treatment, his skin was completely cured.

When Suntae had recovered, the lady told him,

"Actually, I had a son. He went into the army and I never heard from him again. I am not even sure if he is still alive. I have some farmland but with the help of neighbors I barely make a living from farming. If I had money, I would ask you to live with me and also pay to have your eyes treated. I am so sorry but I can't take care of you. I have a hard time even taking care of myself. However I will pray for you every day as long as I live. In the future, I hope you will become God's loyal servant who spreads His Word."

She prayed for Suntae holding him in her arms and said farewell for the last time with tears. She stayed by the gate watching as long as she could see the boy walking away.

Suntae was very thankful for God's grace in all the good that had come to him. Without God's love and care, he would not have met such a kind lady. He gratefully thanked God for everything that had happened to him. He thanked God for letting him survive through the war as well as the times of starving and freezing and also for making him into the brave leader among the beggars who survived through the rough times of this world without becoming a pickpocket or gangster.

Even though I walk through the valley of the shadow of death, I will fear no evil, for you are with me; your rod and your staff, they comfort me.   **Psalm 23:4**

Suntae started to pray, "Dear God who has given me the breath of life. Please give me a fresh new start just like the blades of grass coming out from the ground. Please give me the strength of the buds now coming to life on the branches of trees which look as though they are dead. In my life also bring a new springtime. Make me into one who brings light and hope to the blind, the hopeless, and the poor."

Since that day, Suntae has always prayed before he slept or ate, even when eating from his beggar's can, remembering the unforgettable love the old lady had shown him.

Chapter 11

The Masseur Boy
Who Played the Flute

It was a day like any other. Suntae was begging from door to door, walking down a shaded alley around the marketplace. Suddenly, somebody approached and caught his two arms, putting him inside a van. There were some thirty other beggars inside the vehicle. At that time, the government ordered that beggars be arrested and kept in orphanages or prisons. He trembled all the way in the vehicle, thinking 'Are they going to kill me?'

Fortunately, they were being taken to a child and youth center in western Busan. It was a temporary housing facility for child beggars. After the children were given remedial training to fit their own situation, they were sent to the appropriate orphanage or site. There were twelve sections in the center. Those kids with a good record and disposition were sent to the first four divisions, while beggars with bad behavior and a record of running away after serving in heavy labor at the institution were sent to locations on uninhabited islands. Suntae's life at the center exhibited very good conduct and he went to church every Sunday. One day, the superintendent and the office director called in Suntae and asked, "Suntae, which orphanage do you want to go to?" He had waited for this question for a long time, and he answered, without any hesitation,

"I want to go to an orphanage that can provide me with a proper education."

Several days passed, they called him in again to inform him that there was an institution at Songdo in Busan for blind orphans named the Lighthouse.

"That orphanage provides education, so study as hard as you can to become a great man." Not only did it house blind and deaf orphans, the institution also served as a school.

Four days later, Suntae arrived at his new orphanage with his counselor from the center. Suntae was warmly welcomed at the office on the second floor where they received the two sheets of information about Suntae.

"You are such a smart boy! Study hard at this school and make your dreams come true," said Rev. Duk-Hong Lee, who had served as the principal of the Seoul National School for the Blind and the Lighthouse School for the Blind. A few days later, he was sent to another school for the blind in Gimhae. At this school Suntae finally learned to read Korean Braille from Shin-Gyung Han, a sweet-natured teacher who was like a mother to him.

Meanwhile, Seoul National School for the Blind moved back to Seoul from Gimhae, along with all the orphans and the principal. For a while, the school had had to move to Gimhae away from the Korean War zone. so Suntae was shipped back to the Lighthouse in Songdo. However, he found that the school had changed a lot. For instance, the school staff members brutally abused students, and nobody could stop or change this situation. Even worse, the staff and teachers drank together late into the night ordering blind students to massage them. At the end of a year, the teachers used to throw a party and evaluate the students, one by one. Teachers praised those students who brought a loaf of bread, pairs of socks, or other small presents after they visited their house on weekends, while they sneered at Suntae because he had brought no present whatsoever.

"Your grades are terrible. All you do is make trouble. Why don't you make your living as a masseur? You will have to thank God if you don't starve to death."

Suntae became furious. He ran to the beach near the orphanage and cried his eyes out.

Suntae shouted at the waves.

"God, am I really hopeless, just like the teacher described me? If there is no hope for me, then I would drown myself in the sea right now!"

Then, came the voice of God mixed with the sound of the night sea.

"You don't need to worry. I have overcome the world. You are my beloved son. I will help you."

Suntae was deeply convinced that it was the voice of God that encouraged him to make a new resolution for his life. He set himself straight, and came back to the orphanage.

On his way back to the dormitory, Suntae encountered the dorm supervisor, Mr. Yang, who bluntly asked, "Where did you go?" However, Mr. Yang no longer frightened Suntae.

"I went out to pray to God," answered Suntae, and he went to bed and fell asleep. After that day Suntae wanted spend all his time studying, but Mr. Yang demanded that Suntae massage him all day long. He even slapped Suntae's face when he thought Suntae didn't massage hard enough. When summer vacation started, a teacher who didn't like the way Suntae was being treated said, "Do you want to work as a masseur and earn money in Songdo?" Suntae's answer was definitely 'yes', because he was desperate to earn money for further study. It was usual that juniors should be punished if they made money as a masseur before graduating seniors. Yet, the teacher gave his word that he would take full responsibility for the consequences and bought him a bamboo flute that masseurs need to play to attract customers. "Suntae, you should make money during this summer vacation."

Every night, Suntae walked around residential areas, hotels, and downtown, shouting,

"Sir, would you like a massage? Please get a message!"

Suntae's massage service became popular gradually. He even had as many as four customers a night. If his goal was just to make enough money to live off, then he could have lived like this for the rest of his life. However, first he saved money for his study and church offering, and then, he used the rest of the money to buy snacks for his friends. During those days, he promised himself, 'Even though I can make a good living as a masseur, I will never rely on this skill as my lifetime job. It is against my faith since I learned this skill through Mr. Yang's exploitation of making me give him a massage every night.'

Massage customers were mostly those who came to drinking parties in the red light district and after drinking too much wanted a massage. It made Suntae determined to walk away from the job as a masseur because he didn't want to spend the rest of his life in those kind of places.

Two and half years passed, and Suntae finally finished his elementary graduation examination. He wanted to leave the Lighthouse. The facility for blind children had become a lawless place, along with violence and inhumane treatment.

He decided to make his way to the Seoul School for the Blind for his next education in junior high school. Schools in Busan were not the heaven Suntae had hoped for. During his school years in Busan, Suntae always asked himself, 'Where can I find true happiness?'

He found the answer; the truly happy are those who look forward to the future while enduring present difficulties, and who rise higher with gratitude for that future; they make their own happiness.

Chapter 12

One Empty Promise after Another

After many ups and downs Suntae finally got into the middle school of Seoul School for the Blind. Suntae had to study on the floor without a desk for more than a month due to his late registration. He barely made the entrance exam on time, so he had to rush through the exam. Also, even though he passed the exam, the Busan School sent the registration document late. After sending several letters of complaint to the Busan School, finally the paperwork came and Suntae officially entered the school at last. 'I will finally get a proper education,' thought Suntae, with hope. At that time, he couldn't imagine the other obstacles that would be waiting for him at his new school.

The Ministry of Education supported the students' living expenses for the boarding school, but the students had to pay their own tuition every three months. Luckily, Suntae belonged to the Busan Welfare Foundation for Blind Children. They were supposed to support his education financially, but they didn't send the money promised to him.

His homeroom teacher humiliated Suntae in front of the whole class for not paying tuition. Suntae begged the school to allow him to visit the

Busan School to get the money, nevertheless, the school always refused his request and created more trouble for him every day.

Both blind and deaf students attended the Seoul School for the Blind. They shared the same school building, cafeteria and dormitory. There was always a tension between the blind and the deaf. The deaf students bullied classmates who were blind or had visual impairments. When Suntae tried to cross the school field after class and head toward the dormitory, the deaf students used to take away his bag and push him into a drainage ditch. Also many times they would take away or even spit on the blind students' food.

The blind students could not do anything to protect themselves from their deaf classmates since they could not see what was happening around them. The deaf students would run away so quickly from the scene that they never got caught by their teachers. The blind students could not bear it anymore. One day, they all gathered together to come up with a plan to defend themselves.

"Let's cut off the electricity at night while all the deaf students are sleeping. Then we can attack them in the darkness."

All the blind students agreed to the plan.

Finally, the night of revenge had arrived. The visually impaired students turned off the master switch for the electricity. As soon as the lights went out, the blind students ran into the room and beat up the deaf students with their canes. The deaf students could not communicate with each other in the darkness since they could not speak nor hear, or use sign language. They were beaten up without any chance to fight back.

After that day, the blind students always carried a cane with them not knowing when the deaf students might try to get revenge. As the group fights occurred often, the school had to split into two separate schools: a school for the blind and a school for the deaf.

One semester had passed.

Suntae failed his massage class which prepared students for the most suitable job avail-able to the blind in Korea at that time. In fact, he never really wanted to learn how to give a proper massage because he promised himself that he would not make a living by rubbing other people's bodies. Since Suntae felt for several reasons that he did not belong in the school, he was confused about his future. He made several attempts to get an education to prepare him for the wider world, but nothing worked out as he had hoped.

"Dear God. I don't think this is the right place for me. Please help me to transfer to a school that will fit me better. It's hard to bear the abuse given out by the teachers and upper classmates. Please save me from this place."

Every day at daybreak, Suntae prayed with tears under the old ginkgo tree near the dormitory.

"Is there any other place where I could study? I want to be away from here. Please lead me to an appropriate school without abuse or massage classes."

Suntae went out to pray crying sorrowfully whether the day was too cold or too hot, even when it snowed or rained. Despite his efforts, there was no change in his life. He had no place to go. Nobody offered him a place to stay. Even worse, he had no money. 'Why is there nothing for me? Isn't there someplace in the world for me?' Suntae went to one of the lay pastors whom he knew and cried for help, "I cannot stay in this school anymore. Please help me."

Surprisingly, the lay pastor answered,

"I have good news for you. The missionary pastor, Ahn-Jun Kwak, is looking for a smart young boy with visual impairment. He came from America a long time ago. Pastor Kwak wants to pay for the education for a bright boy like you to become a leader."

Suntae couldn't believe what he had just heard.

"But under one condition. You must study the Bible. Is that okay for you, do you want to meet him?"

Right after that conversation, they visited pastor Kwak's house. After an interview, the missionary exclaimed to the lay pastor, "This is the boy I was looking for!"

"Study hard and become a pastor when you grow up," said the missionary pastor with a big welcome for Suntae. At that time, the Seoul School for the Blind became a hot social issue when the whole school caught typhoid after going on their picnic. They must've eaten rotten food prepared by the school. This incident made the headlines of the newspapers at that time. Every student got the typhoid except Suntae. He took this chance to apply to leave the school. At last, Suntae was able to leave the Seoul School for the Blind as he had so earnestly prayed for over the past few months.

> *See, I am doing a new thing! Now it springs up; do you not perceive it? I am making a way in the wilderness and streams in the wasteland.* **Isaiah 43:19**

With the missionary's help, Suntae registered for math and English classes at an institute in Jongro, Seoul. Even though Suntae studied hard at the institute for several months to prepare for his school entrance exam, he did not forget to read the Bible as he had promised. Suntae had many difficult moments but he always tried to think positively looking to the future. He promised himself he would never stop studying until he would get accepted at a regular school for non-disabled, normal students.

Part 3
New Hope Sprouts Wings

Chapter 13
Bittersweet Days
at a Regular School

Suntae sent off applications to several middle schools. The first reply came from Soongsil Middle School. With excitement, he visited the middle school which was under Principal Suk-Ahn Kim's guidance the next early morning. The principal and all the teachers wholeheartedly welcomed Suntae but asked with doubt, "Are you confident that you can study with non-disabled students? We don't have facilities for the blind, not to mention Braille books."

"I will do my utmost. I will put my full devotion into study. I was taught that nothing is impossible with my Holy Father"

Teachers replied, "You are smart and have strong faith. How about taking the entrance exam for this school?"

He had been waiting this moment for his whole life. He willingly accepted.

"Yes. I will do my best. I will take the test."

And he passed, fairly and squarely.

'Now I am a proud student of Soongsil Middle School, a prestigious school with a long and proud history.'

He sang a hymn to thank his Father in heaven:

God's great grace it has brought us all this way in faithfulness
God's unbounded love which sought us He can tongue of man express
His strong hand is watching over us whether sleeping or awake
He makes all things pleasant for us in the Lord for Jesus' sake

God renews our failing powers with His might from day to day
And in mercy on us showers Grace sufficient for the way
Though the loveless streets be dreary, harsh, and bleak the mountain ways
We shall walk and no be weary clasp His hand and sing His praise

His heart was overwhelmed with joy as he is just about to open a
new chapter of his life as a middle school student, leaving all the suffering
and abuse that he endured in Busan behind.

"Even though I have no family to share my happiness, I am deeply
grateful for your grace to let me be accepted into this wonderful
Christian school."

He felt so lonely as he had no one to share such a good news with,
but the first thing he did was to give all the glory to God for His
guidance.

Studying with non-disabled students turned out to be much more
difficult than Suntae had expected. There was neither Braille book nor
customized facilities for the blind. The teachers also were ·confused as
they had no experience teaching a blind student before.

Suntae was about to start his school life with 3000 students blessed
with normal eyesight. He strengthened his will that he would overcome
all the difficulties and be successful. His fellow students wholeheartedly
helped him achieve his dream.

After class was over, his classmates read their notes aloud for Suntae so that he could take notes in Braille. That even continued after school into the evening hours. All the textbooks also needed to be transcribed into Braille by Suntae himself. His fingers were bruised, yet he was happy.

Suntae studied his books until 1 a.m. with his friends and woke up early to pray to God at the morning service at the Freedom Church. Then he would begin a new day at school. He had a tight schedule since working hard was the only way to catch up with normal students and perform at the same level. For Suntae, everything was a miracle granted by God but at the same time also an obstacle. He did not allow adversity to discourage him. Every day, Suntae renewed his resolution that in order to become God's able servant, first, he had to endure and work hard to compete with normal students.

Whenever Suntae faced frustration and difficulties, Jung-Du Lee, his teacher always stood by Suntae to encourage and support him.

Gym and art class were especially difficult for a blind student like Suntae. However, Suntae refused to be exempted or given special treatment and decided to take exams for the two subjects. One day, for gym class physical test all students had to run a marathon to Namsan Mountain.

"Suntae, given your situation, you can stay behind in the classroom while the others are taking the test. I will give you an average score through special consideration."

"No way, teacher. I will take the test like all the other students. Please give me a chance. Would you just ask two other students to run beside me? Then I will finish the marathon."

The teacher reluctantly agreed, and Suntae completed the marathon as one of the early finishers.

In art class, the test for Suntae had to draw a picture with color pencils using his imagination. He gained confidence through the support of his friends. Many students carried his schoolbag and walked together arm-in-arm to guide Suntae to the bus station after school.

Suntae endeavored to return the love shown by his friends. Just as he won the respect of his fellow beggars leader in Busan, he spent his middle and high school years as a recipient of his friends' respect and admiration.

Suntae's dream and goal was to continue his studies in college and seminary and eventually to achieve a degree in the US and serve his rest of the life as a clergyman and religious leader. He was willing to give up his life for his dreams. This strong desire had allowed him to overcome all obstacles including his disability.

However, his hope was dashed overnight, when he was a senior in high school. After the military coup in 1961, the military government pushed for educational reforms. As a result, all the seniors in high school were required to take a national examination for college education.

The change kept him on his toes. He studied day and night to get into college. Suntae applied to take the national college entrance exam and put all his energy into preparing for this big day. After two weeks, his application was rejected on the grounds that according to the new educational law and policy, visually disabled students could not qualify to take the examination. When Suntae was notified of this law by his teacher, he felt like he was about to faint. All his hopes and dreams were shattered overnight. As the military dictatorship was in power, no one could dare to speak out against the government's policies. Protesting against the government meant putting oneself into danger. Suntae cried all night in desperation and prayed in tears to God.

"Father, what should I do to bear this trial? Why am I put in such adversity? Now I feel that everything is beyond my reach."

Then he heard the Father's voice.

"Suntae, I have saved you from death and protected you for so long. I will never abandon you. Don't back down. Just fight for it, and you will be victorious."

Suntae sang a hymn, encouraged by his Heavenly Father.

Standing on the promises of Christ, my King!
Through eternal ages let His praises ring
"Glory in the highest!" I will shout and sing
Standing on the promises of God, my savior
Standing, standing, I'm standing on the promises of God

Standing on the promises that cannot fail!
When the howling storms of doubt and fear assail
By the living Word of God I shall prevail
Standing on the promises of God, my savior
Standing, standing, I'm standing on the promises of God

Chapter 14

No One Can Clip My Wings

After early morning prayers, Suntae and his homeroom teacher went to the principal's office. He confidently said to the principal,

"Please leave this matter to me. I will solve it by myself. You and the teachers can help me by praying."

For the next three months, everyday Suntae went to the chief superintendent's office in the Ministry of Education begging for permission to take the exam. Every time he visited, the superintendent and workers mocked him. Suntae was not discouraged, rather, it made his will stronger.

Suntae still could not get the permission that would allow him to take the entrance exam after thirty-two visits to the Ministry of Education. He had only three more days until the exam but there seemed to be no possibility to take it.

That night Suntae prayed to God desperately.

"O, God. What should I do? I visited thirty-two times, but I still could not get consent. I only have three days left. If I lose this chance, I will also lose my hope and dreams. I will become a useless person."

Suntae heard the same voice and message as before.

"Fight till the end, then you will win."

As Suntae heard God's voice, he decided to take a knife with him to the superintendent to show how serious he was. He made up his mind that he would beg the superintendent three more times to allow him to take his college entrance. If he didn't accept this request, then the poor, visually disabled Suntae resolved he would kill the superintendent himself. Suntae believed that his radical action would send a significant message to the world so that the other blind students might have better chance to get a higher education in the future. Suntae thought as long as his death could pave the way for a new bright hope for the young blind, he would sacrifice his life to bring justice for the disabled in society.

Early the next morning, Suntae ran to the Education Ministry office with a knife next to his chest and grabbed the superintendent's arm. The superintendent shouted, "Stop annoying me! I will not change my answer! The law clearly states that blind students cannot go to university!" Then he slapped Suntae's face and even kicked him hard. Without hesitation, Suntae took out his knife and fought back yelling, "Unless we solve this problem here and now, we shall die together!" As soon as the superintendent saw the knife he ran away. Actually the other workers in the building also hid themselves quietly. They must've been scared of getting stabbed by the blind student who was whirling a knife in the air. At that time there was a group of newspaper reporters in the building. As they listened to Suntae's story with sympathy, they applauded Suntae's brave act.

"You did well. There is no one in this office now. We will take you to the Secretary of Education."

Suntae confidently went to visit the Secretary of Education.

Alone he couldn't have gotten past the armed guards to meet the government minister, but now Suntae could since he was protected by the reporters walking all around him.

As Suntae entered the Secretary's room he shouted loudly,

"Please allow visually impaired students to take the University Entrance Examination! You must give us a chance!"

When the Secretary heard about Suntae's situation for the first time, he gave Suntae a special exception to be able to take the exam. Workers at the Education Minister's office tried to lead Suntae to another room by dragging his arm. However, Suntae couldn't believe what had just happened. He refused to leave the room until he got the cabinet minister's official seal on the document of dispensation. As he promised, the Secretary had to put the official seal on the document as soon as possible to assure Suntae and allay his fears. After Suntae made sure his document was correctly completed, he went to the other room to finish the official procedures.

One kind worker gave Suntae encouragement by grabbing his arm. She said, "You are so brave. You really worked hard so you deserve it." She held Suntae's hand to lead his way as if Suntae was her boyfriend. (45 years later, Suntae met the kind worker by chance. Her name is Pung-Ja Lee currently serving at Seoul's Somang Church as a senior deaconess.)

For though the righteous fall seven times, they rise again, but the wicked stumble when calamity strikes.   **Proverbs 24:16**

After conquering a mountain of obstacles and barriers, Suntae was able to finally take the University Entrance Exam. Later, he read a newspaper article recounting this most surprising victory and that healed Suntae's bruised heart.

The headline of the article was "High school student Suntae Kim takes University Entrance Exam after 33 visits to the Ministry of Education fighting for justice for the blind." Many other newspapers also covered the story with similar articles and photographs of Suntae protesting, swinging his knife, going into the Secretary's office, and registering to take the entrance exam. People who read the articles came up to Suntae and praised him for his courage. People welcomed him wherever he went and even offered him free meals and a place to sleep. Suntae became famous overnight because of his protest.

> *The Lord brings death and makes alive; he brings down to the grave and raises up. The Lord sends poverty and wealth; he humbles and he exalts.* 1 Samuel 2:6-7

Suntae had been dispirited by his suffering and despair, the likes of which no one else could imagine. He felt he was fighting against the world all by himself and his heart was filled with harrowing pain. But in the end, through his triumph he reaffirmed his faith in God quoting the lyrics of the hymn, "If, On a Quiet Sea."

> *If, on a quiet sea, toward heaven we calmly sail,*
> *Blest be the tempest, kind the storm,*
> *With grateful hearts, O God, to Thee,*
> *We'll own the favoring gale*
>
> *But should the surges rise, and rest delay to come,*
> *Blest be the tempest, kind the storm,*

Which drives us nearer home
Soon shall our doubts and fears all yield to
Thy control; Thy tender mercies shall illume
The midnight of the soul

Teach us, in every state, to make Thy will our own;
And when the joys of sense depart, To live by faith alone.

Suntae's dream came true when he courageously took the exam and was accepted into Soongsil University. Thirty-three attempts at knocking down the brick wall had opened up a door of endless possibilities for Suntae.

Chapter 15

Chapter 15
A Faith Built on Sharing
& Serving Others

'Which subject would be most helpful for me for my further study in college to become a pastor and minister?' Suntae pondered over this question.

Suntae's choice was Western philosophy as it would help to deepen his understanding about God. Not only that, he had learned philosophy as wisdom and knowledge, and eventually he studied the subject of philosophy as a means to pursue the truth.

Then you will know the truth, and the truth will set you free.
John 8:32

Every time he read his Bible he wondered how he could really know 'the truth' spoken of in John 8:32. He wondered how the truth could make himself, who could not see and did not own anything, free.

'I've found the answer! I can't understand God without studying philosophy. I need to think over the sufferings of humanity as a means of understanding God.'

With this realization, he put all his efforts into his studies at Soongsil University.

He poured all his energy into his academic work just to keep up to earn the required semester credits. However, as Suntae planned for his life before and after graduation, he came to the conclusion that study alone was not enough.

'To walk the path of a religious leader, I should be committed to not only academia, but also to volunteer work.'

In pursuit of his belief, he volunteered as a teacher for students at Sunday school in Haebang (Liberation) Church.

After getting off the bus from his campus it took about 50 minutes of hiking to get to Haebang Church located on a high hill. He had to encounter so many obstacles along the way. Sometimes he fell into the ditches beside the street, or was elbowed by bicycle rides, and many times he walked into electric poles, but Suntae endured all these difficulties believing these trials were training for him to become a good pastor.

"I'm so sorry it is so much trouble for you to come all this way, but we cannot offer you meals because our church is financially strained."

"Don't worry about that. I can take care of myself."

During those post-war times, poverty was rampant, and evident even in churches. Suntae used to live on a piece of bread for lunch when staying at church to take part in the young adult meeting. He had to skip breakfast because the dormitory only offered breakfast after his departure time. He had to wake up and leave the dormitory no later than 7 a.m. Nevertheless, it didn't matter to Suntae. Living a humble, sacrificial life was one of the utmost virtues necessary to become a servant of God so he looked at it positively.

Suntae, who didn't have any money, decided to save money by eating fewer meals so that he could spend the money on things he needed more. He used to fast, only drinking water 1 or 2 times a day, and sometimes fasted for 2 or 3 days during a time of special prayer.

In this way fasting brought Suntae closer to God. In return, God granted him a strong body to endure these painful fasts without serious sickness or other hindrance. Fasting was a way to practice self discipline and strengthen self-control to guard oneself against greed and vanity.

He used the money he saved up for a month by skipping meals to give an offering to church, for bus fare, or to buy treats for the children he was teaching at church. The happiness and joy of sacrificing to serve others was great beyond description.

He spent all day Sunday at church as a volunteer teacher and went back to his dormitory late at night. He was exhausted from starving as he skipped meals all day, no one giving him even a bowl of noodles, but he felt satisfied.

Since middle school days Suntae hardly ever had a good night's sleep in order to transcribe his textbooks in Braille and complete his homework assignments which took many hours. His great hope for the future helped him to overcome his lack of sleep. Later on, this strong patience and endurance enabled Suntae to carry on with his volunteer work.

He gained strength from the Book of Isaiah.

Even youths grow tired and weary, and young men stumble and fall; but those who hope in the Lord will renew their strength. They will soar on wings like eagles; they will run and not grow weary, they will walk and not be faint. **Isaiah 40:30-31**

Ten minutes walk away from the back gate of the school, there was a village where there were about 80 teenage lepers. It was only by sheer coincidence that Suntae discovered them. After experiencing children who hung on to his arms longing for affection and care, he realized that there were so many children who needed to be cared for and fed.

After that, Suntae spent just half a day at church and the rest at the village. He read to the leper children from his books and taught hymns and God's Word. He gave out treats to the children and held Sunday school for them.

One day, Suntae got love letters from high school girls in the leper town. Even some girls visited his university in groups and said "Teacher, we missed you!" Unfortunately, all the love letters and affection for him was inappropriate for Suntae since the pure intention of his voluntary work would be compromised.

'My volunteer service here is doing more harm than good. If I continue it only for my own satisfaction, not with true altruism, then all my dreams and hopes will be shattered.'

Then he made the decision to gradually stop working there. He had to pursue the higher goal of serving God.

At that time, one college friend contacted Suntae out of the blue.

"There is a group of people who need your help in Bongcheun Dong. How would feel about us helping out with a Sunday school and a youth meeting there?"

"Of course, I would be more than happy to help them."

As Suntae heard from his friend, Shingwang Church was a very poor church, located in a ghetto neighborhood. All the residents there belonged to the lowest income group and lived in huts made of mud. Although Suntae was not really in a position to help others, he answered God's calling by serving at the church and sacrificing his time to help them.

> *Do nothing out of selfish ambition or vain conceit. Rather, in humility value others above yourselves, not looking to your own interests but each of you to the interests of the others.*
>
> **Philippians 2:3-4**

Chapter 16

To Meet an Angel

"The Shingwang Church building has just been demolished by the City Hall's decision. It turns out the building was unauthorized."

It was shocking news.

"What did you just say? The church was demolished?"

Although Suntae wanted to go right away to help them, he hesitated since his graduation thesis was due soon. Despite his worries about graduation, he hurried to make his way to the church site. He didn't know what to say when he faced the empty land where the church used to stand. All he could do was to pray with the other sisters and brothers from the church asking God for help in the midst of their despair.

He searched for an answer to the question: 'How can I help Shingwang Church?'

Nothing came to mind, simply because like others he had no money to help he was one of the poorest of the poor. At that moment, all he had was the tuition for his final semester and dormitory expenses given by a missionary. After long consideration, Suntae made up his mind.

'I will donate my school tuition for the reconstruction of the church.'

That was a painful decision for Suntae. Perhaps on parr with

Abraham's decision to give up his only son, Isaac, as a burnt offering for God.

> *Give, and it will be given to you. A good measure, pressed down, shaken together and running over, will be poured into your lap. For with the measure you use, it will be measured to you.*
>
> **Luke 6:38**

Afterwards, he went back to the empty church site with the money. Suntae and church members gathered the bricks left behind when the building was demolished and built a small place for worship.

Now that he had given up his tuition, Suntae was forced to spend his last semester as an unregistered student. As expected, he received reminder letters from the university administration office and the dean of students. Under constant pressure, Suntae tried to gather money for his tuition even by selling his cherished books to his juniors, but the money was not even close to being enough.

One day the dean of students called in Suntae. "Studying without paying tuition is the same as stealing others' belongings. You will be expelled unless you pay your tuition right now!" On top of this threat, the dean even swore at him.

"I've spent all my money as an offering to build a new church. Please give me several more days, and I will prepare my tuition fee as soon as possible. I give my word to you so please trust me." Suntae politely, yet desperately appealed to him.

"You idiot, does it make sense to donate your money for a new church? You'll be expelled unless you pay the tuition!" The dean of students yelled in his face, saying he should make sure to pay the money as soon as possible.

How could Suntae raise enough money to continue his study? His mind went blank. Suntae decided to start his massage service again, though it was the last thing he wanted to do. Giving massages was the only thing he could do to earn money in a few weeks and graduate.

Without telling anyone, Suntae went to a wealthy part of the city. Masseurs usually wear formal clothes to show respect to their customers. Suntae, however, did not have any nice clothes and so just carried his masseur's flute wearing his school uniform.

Usually, people heard a masseur's flute and loudly called the masseur from their home. Hearing them call, the masseur went to the house and got paid after providing the massage service. People called to Suntae to come in, but turned him back when they saw that he was a student in school uniform. For five days in a row, he couldn't get any customers. Out of desperation, Suntae prayed to God as always he did whenever he faced difficulties.

"O Lord, help me! Time is running out. Unless I make money within a couple of days, I will be expelled. All my hopes and dreams to work for you will be gone. Please! Help me!"

Soon after the desperate prayer, Suntae was walking along street at night, blowing his flute sadly. His heart was overwhelmed with sorrow. Even the sorrowful tune of his flute made him feel even more melancholy. Suddenly, he heard the voice of an old man calling him.

"Masseur, please come in."

As Suntae came in, the old man asked, "Are you really a student?" Maybe the man saw the school badge on his uniform.

"Yes. I'm in my final semester at Soongsil University."

The man offered him a hot cup of cocoa and sweet potato. Suntae thankfully ate what the man offered and massaged the old man to the best of his ability. During the massage, they talked about many things in their lives. The old man talked about his childhood.

"I am a devoted Christian who fled from North Korea. I had lived near Soongsil University in Pyongyang. Now I am running a business producing glass for construction. Why do you work as a masseur late at night like this?"

"To be honest, I need to make money for my tuition. I got the money from a missionary but I donated it all for a new church."

Then, the old man, kindly asked, "How much do you need?" He generously gave Suntae more than he needed for the tuition, saying, "Please become a great man in the future."

"Sir, thank you. Thank you so much." Suntae bowed repeatedly.

"Please allow me the honor to know your name. I will make sure to pay back the money."

The man, however, never told his name to Suntae. With the kind old man's help, Suntae could pay his tuition and had a little left over to give as a offering of thanks at Shingwang Church.

Be not dismayed whatever betide,
God will take care of you;
Beneath His wings of love abide,
God will take care of you.

Through days of toil when heart doth fail,
God will take care of you;

When dangers fierce your path assail,
God will take care of you.

All you may need He will provide,
God will take care of you;
Nothing you ask will be denied,
God will take care of you.

No matter what may be the test,
God will take care of you;
Lean, weary one, upon His breast,
God will take care of you.

God will take care of you,
Through every day, over all the way;
He will take care of you,
God will take care of you.

Chapter 17

The Promise
with God

Suntae's final semester was coming to an end. Soon the days of hopeful yet painful moments of his four years of college would become precious memories. After taking the final graduation exams, a new chapter of his life would begin. As it was time to leave the stable and settled situation of being a university student behind, Suntae felt an overwhelming sense of anxiety during the final week of graduation exams and commencement ceremonies. The school regulations stated that all students must leave their dormitory within two weeks after graduation. As he could not afford even a small room, Suntae had no choice but to become a homeless person on the streets.

"God, I am an angel without a home. I don't even have a small room to sleep in. Where shall I go?" Every day Suntae prayed to God about this even when he was studying for the exam. Towards the end of the exam period, one of his college seniors who had graduated a year earlier made him a gracious offer.

"I have a small house in Bongcheon. What would you say about living with me?"

That was great news for Suntae for which he was thankful.

"I would be delighted, my dear alumni."

After the exam, Suntae moved to his friend's house with only a few books and clothes. There were two small heated rooms in the house. A poor preacher's family lived in one room for free and the other room was shared by Suntae and his college senior. However, one day his friend shouted at him angrily, "I let you live in my house. From now on why don't you pay for the food?" From that day the friend never paid for the food or household expenses, leaving penniless Suntae in the difficult position of coming up with the living cost for two people if he kept on living there. Under this circumstance, Suntae still thanked the Lord for what he had by singing hymns.

The Lord is my shepherd
And I am his sheep
He leads me to the place where heavenly pastures grow
Where living waters gently pass

The Lord is my shepherd
And I am his sheep
He provides me every meal
I need nothing more

At last, the new chapter of Suntae's life had started. He graduated from Soongsil University after four years as a philosophy major and now he had just finished taking the entrance exam for Seminary.

Although he was accepted by the Presbyterian Theological Seminary, Suntae wasn't quite in a mood to celebrate. As always, he had to worry about tuition and dormitory fees.

Suntae wanted to leave his friend's house as soon as possible and move into the dormitory, but it was impossible for him to come up with all the money. As the registration day for the seminary drew closer, he could not sleep at night because of his worries about the payment. If he could not pay the money, all his dreams would come to naught.

Finally, it was the last day for registration. Climbing up the slope, Suntae was crying loudly with his arms around the cross erected on the hill behind his university.

"God, if I can't pay the money, I have to stop my studies. Then I cannot become your loyal servant. How can I come up with all the money?"

Suntae wept for hours. However, no matter how hard he wept, the money did not miraculously fall into his hands from the sky.

Therefore I tell you, whatever you ask for in prayer, believe that you have received it, and it will be yours.　　　　**Mark 11:24**

After he finished praying, Suntae came down to the university and sat in front of the chaplain's office with a sad look on his face. Then, the chaplain saw the depressed look on Suntae's face and asked,

"Young man, what are you worrying about? What happened to your usual happy face?"

"Dear chaplain, actually today was the last day for seminary registration but I couldn't get the money to pay the tuition."

Desperate Suntae explained to the chaplain his situation that wherever or however he tried he couldn't obtain the necessary money.

"Don't worry. I have a good idea."

The chaplain called on the phone for help to his good old friend, a missionary named Harold Voelkel, whose Korean name was Ho-Yeol Ok. Reverend Voelkel also knew Suntae well from the university. After Rev. Voelkel heard about his desperate situation, he asked Suntae to come to his house right away. The chaplain wished Suntae good luck, praying for him to become an effective pastor.

Suntae didn't even remember how he got to the Voelkel house all by himself. It seemed he was flying and then at the end he kept running although out of breath. When Suntae arrived, Rev. Voelkel graciously handed Suntae money for his tuition without reservation. Suntae ran out of the house without looking back to get to the seminary on time to complete the registration process. He didn't even have time to thank Rev. Voelkel. He had to cross a small muddy stream and run though narrow backstreets. He didn't realize his feet were covered with mud or that his body was bruised from bumping against walls. Luckily, he was able to register at the last minute just before the deadline.

On the first day of seminary when the opening worship was held, students from all over Korea came to the dormitory with their luggage. Though Suntae found a place to stay in the dormitory, he could not stop worrying about food expenses at the school.

"Suntae, I will give you one of my food tickets. Go and eat your lunch."

Some friends took care of him but their help was not enough to get through the whole semester. Sometimes he could eat using a friend's lunch ticket, but that didn't mean he could always live on other people's money. Suntae did not want to pressure any of his friends. At lunch time, while everyone was eating their lunch Suntae would sneak up the mountain near school and he prayed to God instead.

"God, if you let me become a pastor after graduation from the seminary, I will give away more than half of my salary to poor sisters and brothers. In your grace, allow me to have two meals per day and help me graduate from seminary, please."

As Suntae was praying with tears, he would get so hungry that he ate the new buds from the trees on the mountain to relieve his hunger.

"When will I be able to taste warm rice and beef soup? I really want to be able to eat rice-cakes to my heart's content."

On many days Suntae would sneak up to the school rooftop to weep quietly, as he did not want to show his tears to his friends.

So do not worry, saying, 'What shall we eat?' or 'What shall we drink?'
or 'What shall we wear?' **Matthew 6:31**

But seek first his kingdom and his righteousness, and all these things
will be given to you as well. **Matthew 6:33**

One day, one of the school office workers called Suntae. "Suntae, I have good news for you. One American doctor donated 200 dollars for you."

Suntae was surprised to hear the good news. "Donation for me? 200 dollars?" Immediately, he knelt down to thank God for answering his prayer.

"God, I will sacrifice all my life for others when I graduate and become a pastor in the future."

Thanks to the American doctor, Suntae was able to finish the semester without worrying about hunger.

Chapter 18

God's
Unbreakable Love

Suntae, now a young man, was on his second semester of seminary. He was offered several part-time jobs, but he wanted to teach English more than anything. During his school years, he had studied English dilligently wishing to study abroad. He heard there was a Bible study group looking for an English teacher.

Suntae had an interview but couldn't get the job. He was rejected not because of his English ability, but because of his blindness. He was angry at the fact that he wasn't even given a chance simply because he was blind. He hated his situation, thinking that if only one of his eyes were normal, the job would be his.

Suntae cried and called God's name.

And I will do whatever you ask in my name, so that the Father may be glorified in the Son. You may ask me for anything in my name, and I will do it. **John 14:13-14**

Whenever he was in deep sorrow and desperation, Suntae always prayed, reminding the words he read at Sunday school as a boy.

"If you remain in me and my words remain in you, ask whatever you wish, and it will be done for you."   John 15:7

The words of the bible were the only hope he depended on. He kneeled down and prayed. As written in the Book of John, God always stood beside him fulfilling Suntae's needs.

Suntae strongly believed that God was his true father who gave unconditional love and cared for him. That's why whenever he was in trouble, he asked God for the fatherly help to solve all his problems. There was a strong bond of affection between God and Suntae — so strong that it could not be broken. In return, he promised to his Father in heaven that he would dedicate his life, family, and wealth to the church.

Who shall separate us from the love of Christ? Shall trouble or hardship or persecution or famine or nakedness or danger or sword?
                                        Romans 8:35

Neither height nor depth, nor anything else in all creation, will be able to separate us from the love of God that is in Christ Jesus our Lord.   Romans 8:39

Bicycles, hand carts, opened drains, and electric poles — these are very common things we see on the street, but they can be a great danger to those who are visually impaired.

On his second year in seminary, Suntae had a big accident on his way back from bookstore to school. There was no pit in the street on the way to the bookstore. While he was in the bookstore, a big hole was dug up for sewage construction. Suntae walked as usual without expecting to find a hole ahead of him. All of a sudden, he felt his whole body sink and fall. Surrounded by cries of old ladies, he found his forehead and the right eye had been injured by the blade of the shovel on the bottom of the hole.

"Ahhhhh! Somebody help me!"

His body was covered with mud, with blood running down from his forehead and the eye. Someone pulled him out, and soon after, he passed out.

He woke up in the hospital. Doctors sewed nine stitches without anesthesia. The pain was unbearable. Suntae got mad.

'Who on earth dug a hole in the middle of a street?'

He asked his friend to find out who was in charge of digging the hole. "Will you check out who is responsible for this accident?"

A moment later, the friend came back reporting,

"Suntae, Gwang-Jang Church dug the hole to bury water pipes."

Luckily, the chief of the hospital was an elder of the Church. After he heard about the accident, the elder and church members visited Suntae to pray for his full recovery.

Since that day, the church started its missionary work to help the blind to get job trainings and spiritual discipline as well as financial support.

Suntae raised his seminary tuition by working at an orphanage or Sunday school. Sometimes he worked for them without getting paid. Indeed, poverty would be the best word to describe his youthful years. Suntae only had one set of clothes for all four seasons. Some students didn't want to be close to him because of his bad smell.

He was always hungry. While others were eating lunch, he would rather spend his time with God. However, every hungry moment was rewarding for Suntae as God's voice always encouraged him.

"Suntae, I'm with you in every step of your way."

Through His voice, Suntae could know that God is the one who holds him in His arms and endures his pain together, not the one who brings him in pain. God not only weathered the storm by his side, but also helped him to finish the seminary by providing scholarships from unknown donors and charity groups.

During those days, Suntae found his new family at Immanuel Blind Women's Group Home. Blindness was the source of a strong bond between women at Immanuel and Suntae. Blind women would have considered Suntae as their family, too.

'I will volunteer to work for anyone in need of love and companion.'

While serving others, he made detailed plans for his life as a pastor. Suntae made another promise to God — when he could make his own money some day, he would donate it to serve God and others.

"God, give me strength to love many who are in need. Even though I am blind, give me wisdom not to become a short-sighted leader but to become a one who can guide and enlighten others' life."

When Suntae heard the following hymn, he knew that it was the right guidance for his life:

> *Everything brings back to life*
> *when morning sun rises*
> *Let me be the sunshine in this life.*
> *God help me not to waste my life.*
> *Let me be the sunshine in this dark life.*

I will give my mind and soul day and night for God
Let me be the sunshine that shows God's love
God help me not to waste my life.
Let me be the sunshine in this dark life.

Part 4
Sailing on the Wings of Hope

Chapter 19
A Special Honeymoon

During his life at the seminary, Suntae spent most of his hours studying and praying. He was too busy to deal with other matters around him. As they moved closer to graduation, more than half of his classmates had gotten married and some even had children.

Suntae always thought that marriage was a blessing from God. However, for someone penniless and homeless like Suntae, the prospect of marriage and a family was like an elusive rainbow far his grasp.

Nevertheless, Suntae never gave up hope believing that God had a masterplan for all people. Nothing turns out the way people plan, unless it matches with God's intention.

Maybe it was God's plan—there were some girls who thought Suntae, who didn't even have a second set of clothes, was a good future husband.

"Why would girls want to get married to someone like me?"

Although Suntae was flattered, he could not understand them. One afternoon, a friend asked Suntae if he was interested in being set up on a blind date.

"Suntae, there is a girl who wants to meet you. Why don't you meet the girl?"

"No thanks. I never thought of getting married before. But thank you for asking."

Suntae had never before brought the subject of marriage to God in his prayers. That night, he went to church and this time he seriously prayed about marriage.

"Dear God, who have you prepared for me as my future wife? What kind of personality and qualities will she have? Can a humble man like me get married like a normal person?"

As he was praying to God, he clearly realized that God had prepared a wife for him, too.

"I will always obey God's will regardless of what He prepared for me. If God allows and is pleased with this, I will obey."

From that day, Suntae's started to include marriage on his prayer list.

"I get married only once in my life. Who will turn out to be the bride prepared to stand by my side at our holy wedding?"

'I hope my bride looks like my mom, whom I would even risk my life to see again. I also hope she has a kind heart like an angel. Although I have lost my eyesight, I long to see her face just once.'

With all different thoughts running through his head, he kept the following words in his mind as he prayed:

Then the Lord God made a woman from the rib he had taken out of the man, and he brought her to the man. The man said, "This is now bone of my bones and flesh of my flesh; she shall be called 'woman,' for she was taken out of man." That is why a man leaves his father and mother and is united to his wife, and they become one flesh. **Genesis 2:22-24**

As Suntae's graduation drew closer, he was introduced to another girl.

"This girl is talented in music. Most of all, her family has a strong Christian faith. I think you should definitely meet her."

One week later, Suntae finally had a chance to meet the girl alone.

"I am a poor blind man with no house to live in or other earthy possessions. But I am a passenger on a train called faith and trust in God. It is on a journey full of hopes and dreams moving toward the future. I have nothing great to show for now, but I can promise you that I am more confident about my future prospects than anyone else."

Then the girl replied,

"If we are poor then we just need to spend money wisely. We should always be grateful for what God has given us. Don't worry."

Suntae also asked about her faith.

"What would you do if you faced many obstacles to worship God, like a war?"

Suntae continuously asked other similar questions to test her faith. Maybe, he was reflecting on his childhood memories during the war. Without hesitation, she answered his questions.

"No matter what happened, I would choose my faith over my own life."

Suntae was moved by the way she answered. She replied very firmly as if she could die right then for her faith.

'I really want to see her face. What would she look like? Does she look like my mother?'

He fell in love for the first time in his life.

After getting to know each other for awhile, Suntae finally had an engagement dinner with her family. At first, her parents were strongly against their marriage, however, the power of their love for each other won over her parents and their blessing.

Right after their engagement, she went to Immanuel House for Blind Orphans located in Suyu-ri. In order to understand the visually impaired, she had decided that she wanted to be properly trained to gain a deeper understanding. After her 10 months of volunteer work at Immanuel House, they finally got married. When their wedding ceremony was over, the groom, Suntae, told his bride,

"I think it is inappropriate for us to go on our honeymoon to Onyang Hot Springs, Gyeongju or Mt. Sorak like other couples usually do."

"Then, what do you have in mind, darling?"

"I think that we are two people who were linked together by God in a special way. We should spend our honeymoon trip at Immanuel House for Blind Orphans. It would be meaningful to start our new life by helping the orphans there."

Thankfully, Suntae's bride accepted his proposal. When the new groom and bride entered Immanuel House, all the children ran and gave them such big hugs that they fell over.

"Teacher!"

The newlyweds fell on the floor with the children tangled in their arms. At dinner time, the principal asked Suntae,

"Congratulations, but what are you doing here? Why did you choose to come here for your honeymoon?"

Then the bride gave a witty answer,

"I missed the exquisite rice Immanuel House served with their meals. We would not have missed this world famous special rice for anything in the world!"

"Really? Hahaha!"

Everyone broke out into joyful laughter. But Suntae suddenly burst into tears.

"This groom needs more soup! He is seasoning his soup with tears to finish his rice. Please bring him some more soup!"

All of a sudden, the Immanuel Choir members burst into the room to shower them with firecrackers and music to celebrate their wedding.

Suntae's honeymoon started in Immanuel House with the blessing and celebration of blind orphans. It turned out to be a far better experience than having their wedding night at an expensive hotel in some famous tourist location.

Though the fig tree does not bud and there are no grapes on the vines, though the olive crop fails and the fields produce no food, though there are no sheep in the pen and no cattle in the stalls,   yet I will rejoice in the Lord, I will be joyful in God my Savior.

Habakkuk 3:17-18

The young couple's first home was just a small room with a tiny table on the floor. They went to the market and bought two pairs of bowls? one for rice and the other for soup. Sadly the honeymoon ended too soon and Suntae had to go back to the dormitory to finish his graduation exam and dissertation.

At last, it was time for his graduation from seminary. For his graduation, Suntae invited his aunt, who he located after a long search. The same aunt who used to abuse Suntae cursing him to die when he was a small boy. Suntae wanted to show his aunt how he had succeeded with God's help. Also, his plan was to make her repent to God for her actions and be reborn as a new person. There was also one thing that Suntae wanted to thank her for. During the war, if she had taken care of him with love and sympathy when he became visually impaired, then he would not have become the faithful servant of God's light he now was.

If your enemy is hungry, feed him; if he is thirsty, give him something to drink. In doing this, you will heap burning coals on his head.

Romans 12:20

After the graduation ceremony Suntae shook hands with his aunt whom he was reunited with after a long time. He could feel that her hands were drenched with her tears. Suntae forgave his aunt from the bottom of his heart with God's true love. Now with a Master of Divinity degree, Suntae was qualified to become a pastor to become a leader and begin mission work for the visually impaired. Most of all, Suntae thanked God gratefully for guiding and protecting his days at the seminary.

The Lord bless you and keep you; the Lord make his face shine on you and be gracious to you; the Lord turn his face toward you and give you peace. **Numbers 6:24-26**

Chapter 20

The Realization & Answer:'Only God!'

Now Suntae had graduated from seminary and he started to work diligently as an unordained pastor at a church where the members were not disabled. Suntae Kim's new duties were to assist at Sunday services and Sunday school, lead the choir and make various visits. He put his best effort into every duty that was entrusted to him, believing that any work given by God is worthy of his utmost attention and effort. Touched by his diligence, all the members of the church—from children through adults—liked Suntae and followed his leadership.

The only exception was the senior pastor. He used to treat young Suntae with empathy and compassion. The more people started to follow Suntae's leadership, the stronger the senior's jealousy grew. As one just beginning his pastoral work, every day at the church became increasingly uncomfortable for Suntae. One day Suntae heard a hymn during the service and the lyrics perfectly described his situation:

> *"I'm but a stranger here, Heaven is my home;*
> *Earth is a desert drear, Heaven is my home.*
> *Danger and sorrow stand Round me on every hand;*
> *Heaven is my father-land, Heaven is my home."*

'Perhaps this church is not the place of my calling.'

Not being able to endure the situation, Suntae resigned his position and transferred to a different church.

At the new church, he was put in charge of the children and youth ministry. Nevertheless, a similar situation arose with the senior pastor of this new church as well.

'I am certain that I did my best, but why are things getting harder and harder? Perhaps this church isn't right for me either.'

Suntae felt frustrated. Just doing his best did not make things turn out right.

'It would be better if I started a new church myself for the visually impaired.'

It was a very bold decision since Suntae had nothing at all with which to start a new church.

We can make our own plans, but the Lord gives the right answer. People may be pure in their own eyes, but the Lord examines their motives. Commit your actions to the Lord, and your plans will succeed.　　　　　　　　　　　　　　　　　**Proverbs 16:1-3**

'How can I establish a church for the blind?'

He pondered it over and came up with an idea.

'Even though it may be impossible to meet with the President, perhaps I could meet with the Prime Minister at least to request some financial assistance. Then I could charter my own path toward hope.'

The next day, Suntae went to the Capitol Building and begged the security guard to let him meet with the Prime Minister. He went to the Capitol Building for several days, nevertheless, the guards turned him back, giving him excuses like "He went to the Blue House," or "He is in a meeting."

Yet, Suntae did not give up. For several days, as soon as he woke up, he went to the front gate and waited for the Prime Minister.

"Is it you, again!"

"Yes. Is today my lucky day to meet with the Prime Minister?"

Now, Suntae became closer to the guards even exchanging friendly talk. One guard was touched by Suntae's effort and whispered to him to try at the Prime Minister's residence in Samchung Dong.

Taking his advice, he went to the residence early in the morning so that he could meet the Prime Minister on the way to work.

Security was heavier than at the Capitol Building. They didn't even allow Suntae to approach the security office. Suntae waited for a whole day to see the Prime Minister returning home from work. One small loaf of bread was the only thing he had eaten while waiting.

"Who are you? Why are you lingering here all day long? You are suspicious. I will report you to the police. Don't move!"

The guards grabbed his neck with their strong arms.

"I am not here with bad intentions! I promise you I am not a crazy man! I simply need to meet the Prime Minister to get his help realizing my great plan for the future,."

"Take out your national identification card!"

As Suntae did not have that form of I.D. with him. Instead, he showed a student card from the seminary. After checking his card, one policeman said, "You will never have a chance to meet him here. Why don't you go to his personal residence in Chunggu-dong?" He listened very carefully to get the details correct and the next morning, he headed off to Chunggu-dong in search of his residence.

The security guards there humiliated Suntae, swearing and calling him a lunatic.

'If I keep using this strategy, I will never see the Prime Minister. Although I might meet him, I will be kicked out even before I get a chance to speak a word. I should approach the Prime Minister in a different manner.'

Suntae stayed up until late that night writing a letter to the Prime Minister. The next morning, he visited the security office as usual. Finally, one guard showed sympathy towards Suntae.

"I'm so impressed with your valiant effort, that I will contact the secretary's office. But please do not be disappointed if you are unable to see him today."

"Thank you. I really appreciate it."

A moment later, Suntae was allowed into the secretary's office of the Prime Minister for the first time in his life.

"What brought you here?" asked the Secretary".

"I wrote this letter all night. Please grant me a meeting with the Prime Minister."

Suntae pleaded, carefully handing the letter addressed to the Prime Minister.

"He is out now so just leave the letter here, please. I will contact you later."

"Please make sure to contact me."

He had no phone at home so he left the phone number of Immanuel

House. He patiently waited, but never got a call back from the Prime Minister.

He sent a letter of appeal more than 30 times to the President and also the Prime Minister, but unfortunately, he never received any response. All his efforts and hopes went down the drain. Suntae decided that he no longer would expect anything from those in high positions of authority. He was not willing to give up, but rather, decided to keep on trying armed with an even stronger determination. He made a promise to himself that he will never forget: 'No matter how high the mountain is, I will overcome the obstacles through faith—by depending on no one else but God and by entrusting my hopes to the Lord."

After many years, Suntae realized that he has served the country and society in ways that not even the President and Prime Minister were able to. Ironically, perhaps he wouldn't have realized all of his achievements if he had managed to meet with the Prime Minister that day. If he had gotten a little help back then, he would have been satisfied with his smaller victory and just settled for less. Much less.

Later, when Suntae was older and more respected, he was given the honor of meeting with former President Young-Sam Kim.

Chapter 21

The Siloam Mother's Association

Suntae took care of a young blind couple living in Yangdong, a shanty town for the poor. The people in Yangdong lived a hand-to-mouth existence. Their only way to make a living was to beg on the streets, work at a restaurant or cafe, or sell pens and gum on the street. After paying their housing rent on a daily basis, they had almost no money left to eat or live, not to mention to have a gas-heater to warm the house. Instead, people usually had a coal briquette-stove in their room to cook or boil water. This included the young couple that Suntae was taking care of as well.

The blind couple had a baby, but it was challenging for them to take care of her. When the baby was about to become one-year-old, the mother accidently tipped over a boiling kettle from the stove. The boiling water poured onto the baby and ended up killing her on the spot.

News of the horrifying incident broke Suntae's heart.

'I am struggling hard every day to help them. But simply giving my fellow blind brothers and sisters food or a few canes will never solve their problem. How can I empower them to become independent and live on their own?'

He came to the conclusion that he needed to get outside help. He knew that it was beyond his ability. Back then, an interdenominational group called the Siloam Mother's Association was related to the Presbyterian mission's committee for the blind. The group reached out in various ways to help visually impaired people in need.

Suntae pleaded with the Siloam Mothers' Association for help.

"We need your support. Blind people in Yangdong are suffering and living in dire circumstances."

He described in detail the wretched conditions the blind were living under.

"Of course we'd like to help them. It is our duty to help those in need."

Thankfully, the members accepted Suntae's request. Since then, the Siloam Mothers' Association members volunteered to visit the blind in Yangdong; the kind volunteers washed their laundry, provided rice and noodles, and prepared the winter supply of kimchi to make blind people's lives better.

With God's blessing, there was even greater joyful news for the blind. As the Aeneung Church was built nearby, the blind people living in the Yangdong area finally had a church they could attend to worship God every Sunday. Going to church transformed their lives. People started to enjoy daily church life by participating in the choir and youth group. The affection and care provided by the Siloam Mothers' Group brought smiles to their faces. Also because they felt they were a welcomed, integral part of society, the blind started to respect themselves more and gained confidence. The Siloam Mothers' prayers, affection, and care played a significant role in encouraging those who had thought their existence was bleak and miserable.

'The greatest challenge we need to overcome for the blind is to provide them with a church,' thought Suntae.

Witnessing this remarkable transformation, Suntae resolved then and there that he would establish a church for the blind.

'What do I have to do to make this dream come true?'

Suntae's first step was to meet his fellow classmates and friends. They accompanied him to go see Pastor Kyung-Chik Han, the most respected Presbyterian minister in Korea. Pastor Han said that they should pray for peoples blessings rather than simply requesting funds. Pastor Han's support, endorsement and prayer encouraged Suntae and empowered him to every place he could to build awareness and receive donations for his new church.

Thanks to the inexhaustable help and support from Suntae's fellow pastors, at last, by the grace of God Suntae was able to establish a new church—the United Church in Korea for the Blind. From the start, the church went through financial difficulties, since the church spent most of its money as assistance for the visually impaired.

While making numerous visits to churches to appeal for contributions, someone introduced Suntae to Pastor Emeritus Se-Jin Kim, and Rev. Gi-Won Han, senior pastor of the Dongshin Church. Whenever he had time, Suntae met with them to share the plans for mission he had conceived. They genuinely wanted to support his vision.

"What about starting a formal support group? This group will be a great help in funding the blind mission work."

"I thought the same way. I will serve as the chairperson for the group and you must give all your effort. Suntae, I believe in you," said Rev. Se-Jin Kim.

With their endorsement a support group was formed—and their work was successful beyond belief, even holding the Asia Mission Conference for the Blind. They were able to hold a series of mass rallies and charity concerts that energized citizens of Seoul. On Christmas day, the Dongshin Church held a Christmas Banquet for the blind.

That night, Rev. Se-Jin Kim was greatly moved by the overwhelming support and response to help the blind. He called in Suntae to meet with him privately.

"While you're working on this important task, I want to take care of your family. I would like to give you some money every month as additional support for your family's living expense."

For some years, he kept sending a large amount of money every month for Suntae's family.

However, Suntae never spent a dime of that money on his family as he had promised to God a long time before. He never forgot his desperate prayer to the Lord during his hungry days at the seminary: "Lord, after I graduate from seminary and become your servant, I will give away all I have to help others."

Teach those who are rich in this world not to be proud and not to trust in their money, which is so unreliable. Their trust should be in God, who richly gives us all we need for our enjoyment. Tell them to use their money to do good. They should be rich in good works and generous to those in need, always being ready to share with others. By doing this they will be storing up their treasure as a good foundation for the future so that they may experience true life.

1 Timothy 6:17–19

Chapter 22

Ordained
At Last!

At last Suntae's long-held dream was finally realized in 1973, four years after graduating from seminary. Suntae was ordained a pastor of Seoul Presbytery at the General Assembly of the Presbyterian Church in Korea — a moment of overwhelming gratitude and honor.

'The moment members of the ordination committee laid their hands on my head and prayed, the Holy Spirit warmed my whole body. I was literally immersed in God's unfathomable love and tears of thanks to God fell from my eyes like a shower of rain.'

In the overwhelming moment, the events of his hard, painful past flashed through his mind. Ever since he ran away from his aunt's house more than twenty years before, God had been with Suntae every single step. Jehovah went before Suntae by day in a pillar of cloud, to lead the way, and by night in a pillar of fire, to give Suntae light. God fed him manna. God empowered him to overcome all the adversity and difficulties. God nurtured leadership in Suntae as a minister.

At long last, Suntae received the laying on of hands and was ordained as a pastor. Suntae had always known that the destination of his long journey that God had prepared for him was not to become an orphan, beggar, beggar leader, or masseur, but rather a pastor and servant of God.

There came changes in how he was perceived after his ordination. Suntae's new status enabled him to expand his own mission work, as well as to establish the Blind Evangelical Mission Office within the Evangelism Department of the Presbyterian Church of Korea. Of course to persuade the General Assembly of the Presbyterian Church to add a new mission office for the blind meant overcoming a lot of difficulties.

People not only held onto negative stereotypes about the blind, even worse; society had almost no understanding about their lives. Even after Suntae became a minister, some people said that it would be 'improper' to have blind individuals moving in and out of church headquarters and that they should be prevented from doing so.

Nevertheless, nothing could stop Suntae. He started his leadership of the Blind Evangelical Mission with a desk in a small office inside the Evangelism Department of the Presbyterian denomination.

Your beginnings will seem humble, so prosperous will your future be.
Job 8:7

Soon after, Suntae found that there were not so many ways to help the blind except charity bazaars, music concerts, and special conferences about the blind. Discouraged, Suntae tried to find the answer through prayer to God.

'God, Are there better ways to help blind people? How can I give them hope to live a better life?'

In 1977, Suntae met someone who took him one step further in his mission for the blind. It was home economics Professor Jung-Soon Lee and her only son.

"I'm here to visit Pastor Suntae Kim."

"I am Suntae Kim."

"Pastor, my name is Jung-Soon Lee, a professor at Chungbuk National University."

"It's nice to meet you. What brought you here?"

"Pastor, a few days ago I happened to visit a school for blind children. As I was talking with the children, I saw a white thin film-like membrane covering some of the pupils of their eyes. I thought if this membrane could be removed, the children would be able to see the bright world."

She went on saying, "Since that day, I have prayed every night in search of the way to make this happen. Then, one day, I heard the Lord's voice."

Rev. Suntae was curious to hear her next words. She continued,

"God told me, 'Jung-Soon, my dear daughter. Do all you can to help these children see again.' I was surprised but without hesitation, I answered in obedience to the Lord that I would do what He said. But I am not a doctor and I don't know how to go about doing this. And so I have come to you, Pastor Kim."

Then Jung-Soon handed Suntae a large amount of money, all that she had saved for her only son's wedding.

"I hope this money can start a fund to pay for eyesight recovery surgery for the blind to deliver them from the darkness."

She and her only son willingly donated the money and left.

After a number of consultations with ophthalmologists, the very first eyesight recovery surgery was conducted on a blind man in his sixties. The man's vision was restored to twenty-forty. The medical team was encouraged and a movement to provide eye operations for the visually impaired progressed with positive steps.

The success of the first operation was hailed widely in and out of the church as 'the miracle of Siloam'. Encouraged by this, the medical team and church decided to make this campaign for eye surgery public through the media. That included Christian magazines writing numerous favorable articles about the campaign to provide 'Eye Operations of Love.'

As support and popularity increased, not only churches, but also many people from around the world sent donations for this campaign, and also to pay for medical equipment needed to provide eye surgery on a larger scale.

In the end, professor Jung-Soon Lee's vision and sacrifice served as a seed that grew into this campaign to bring God's light to the blind—physically and spiritually.

I tell you the truth, unless a kernel of wheat is planted in the soil and dies, it remains alone. But its death will produce many new kernels—a plentiful harvest of new lives. **John 12:24**

Lions Club International and many other organizations and groups donated money to help the blind, often with one stipulation: as benefactors they wanted to meet the recipients who would received their help, to see how they would fare after surgery.

In a similar manner, one supporting church asked for the opportunity to hear a testimony from one of the recipients.

"I know that your affection towards the recipients is just as strong as our desire to send our recipients to you. Yet, seeing the world with their eyes is still uncomfortable for these people. Attending a meeting with a large group of people would be confusing and embarrassing for them. Please understand their difficulties."

As a blind person himself, Suntae had to explain to people how confusing an experience it would be to see the world for the first time after spending many years in darkness. After surgery, the patients needed more help in their daily life, for a much longer time, than they had expected. Readjusting to do simple mundane tasks such as walking the streets, eating meals, and even taking public transportation was an unsettling experience for them. It would not be fair to put them in the public spotlight, as it would be a immense burden on them when they were facing such personal challenges.

That is perhaps why Jesus said the following in the Book of Matthew:

But when you give to someone in need, don't let your left hand know what your right hand is doing. Give your gifts in private, and your Father, who sees everything, will reward you.

Matthew 6:3-4

Chapter 23

Soo-Cheol's Death

One chilly autumn day, the Dongan Church was having a worship service to help visually disabled brothers and sisters. Reverend Suntae asked a favor of the music teacher of the school for the blind.

"It would be great if a student could sing a hymn in front of the church after the sermon."

"We have a special student who plays the flute very well. How about listening to his flute?"

"Who is that boy?"

"His name is Soo-Cheol Kim. When he was in the 8th grade, he lost his eyesight during surgery to remove a brain tumor. It was such a tragedy for his family. Actually, he was born into a wealthy family. His father is a professor at Busan University and his brothers are honor students at Seoul National University. Currently he is studying Braille at our school for the blind. Sometimes he plays the flute to comfort himself. Though he is an amateur, he can really play beautifully."

"That sounds great. Let him play the flute after the sermon."

That day Rev. Suntae met Soo-Cheol for the first time.

On Sunday Soo-Cheol played his flute in front of 600 members in the church service. In the middle of his performance, Soo-Cheol suddenly fainted and fell to the floor.

Shocked, members of the congregation quickly took Soo-Cheol to the hospital. Later Rev. Suntae heard the devastating news that Soo-Cheol had died in the middle of treatment at the hospital.

"Rev. Suntae, I have terrible news. Soo-Cheol just passed away!"

"That's not possible! What do you mean? He died? Why and how?"

Rev. Kim refused to believe the heartbreaking news. He rushed to the hospital as quickly as possible. He ran into the hospital morgue in disbelief, but all he could find was Soo-Cheo's cold dead body. That night Rev. Suntae and Soo-Cheol's older brother Soo-Deok went to the police station to find out the cause of the tragic death. The investigation continued until the next morning. After the investigation was finished, Rev. Suntae went back to the hospital morgue with a sliver of hope that God might have brought him back to life.

Unfortunately, Soo-Cheol did not stir at all.

"I wish he could have my life. I want to exchange places with him."

Rev. Suntae mourned all through the night sorrowfully.

During the funeral service, Rev. Suntae read out the investigation report in front of the coffin. He also made a promise to Soo-Cheol.

"Soo-Cheol, from now on I will practice the flute everyday to give glory to God and to remember you. I feel so sorry for you as your life was cut short. I hope you are happy in heaven, a place with no brain tumors or blindness."

After burying the poor boy in the cold cemetery, Rev. Suntae had a hard time taking his leave and heading home.

Since that day, Rev. Kim practiced the flute everyday in his office. He practiced so hard that he kept playing the flute even in his dreams. It must have been almost a year since Rev. Suntae started practicing the flute after Soo-Cheol's death. In memory of Soo-Cheol, he played a flute solo during a Wednesday service.

The first hymn he played was 'Amazing Grace.'

Amazing grace. How sweet the sound. That saved a wretch like me.
I once was lost, but now am found. Was blind, but now I see.

Through many dangers, toils, and snares I have already come.
'Twas grace hath brought me safe thus far. And grace will lead me home.

When we've been there ten thousand years. Bright shining as the sun.
We've no less days to sing God's praise Than when we first begun.
Amen.

Since then, Rev. Suntae has played the flute after his sermon every now and then. And whenever he plays the flute, Rev. Suntae pictures Soo-Cheol in his mind, playing the flute joyfully in heaven above free from all worries and pain.

'Now Soo-Cheol is in heaven but he lives on in our memory, giving inspiration to many brothers and sisters.' Rev. Kim was one of those brothers who was touched by Soo-Cheol's commitment and sacrifice.

'For whether we live, we live unto the Lord; and whether we die, we
die unto the Lord: whether we live therefore, or die, we are the Lord's.'
Romans 14:8

Chapter 24

The Establishment of Siloam Eye Hospital

A big Christmas charity concert for the visually impaired was held at a local church in December, 1981. For this charity concert, several people who had their eyesight restored through the campaign 'Eye Operations of Love' gave their testimony.

That day the audience which filled the church could not hide their tears after listening to the beautiful music and moving testimonies.

Rev. Suntae Kim prayed,

"God, today we are all gathered here to continue your mission for the visually impaired. Bless us. Show us the miracle of your love."

Each testimony moved people's hearts.

There was one young girl who had never seen the world in her life due to congenital cataracts. She shared her experience of gaining eyesight after four continuous eye operations. When she finished her testimony, the audience filled with tears in their eyes gave her a big round of applause. Her testimony was so touching, that it resulted in an even greater miracle.

The CEO of Goryeo Corporation, Mr. Hwi-Jang Jang, had attended this remarkable concert. He was so touched by the event that he wanted to meet Rev. Suntae Kim privately.

"Rev. Kim, let's build an eye hospital specializing in eyesight recovery surgery. I will share your vision with my fellow businessmen to muster support."

Mr. Jang poured all of his energy into setting up the committee to promote the specialist eye hospital. Not only that, he also searched ceaselessly to find the perfect location for the hospital, as he believed the hospital should be easily accessible to by public transportation to attract people near and far. As Rev. Suntae had always done, he visited his dear mentor, Pastor Han, again to get support as Suntae was about to set off on his dream of building an eye hospital for the blind. After Pastor Han heard the story, he helped Suntae by asking fellow church leaders for some support.

"I always regretted that in my pastoral service I never built a hospital for medical missions. Although we may face many obstacles, we shall overcome them together. Let us build an eye hospital to honor the 100th anniversary of the Korean Church. How about us naming it 'Siloam,' which means 'sent by God'?"

The people on the committee all held each others' hands and with tears prayed fervently for God's blessing. Pastor Han was chosen as the advisor to the committee which helped to push forward their plan of building the Siloam Eye Hospital.

After his hard work of raising enough funds, Mr. Jang was able to purchase the plot of land where the Siloam Eye Hospital currently stands.

In February 1986, the first Siloam Eye Hospital opened its doors at last. Although the hospital was not very large, it was built to bring bright light to the world. Thus through prayer, dreams and preparation the Siloam Eye Hospital opened its doors.

However as the hospital still had financial difficulties, it could barely pay the salary of the medical staff. Due to poor construction, the ceilings leaked, and worse still, the hospital did not have enough equipment to adequately perform eye operations.

Opening the doors of the Siloam Hospital was not an end in itself as it needed to stay open and functional. The hospital was a nonprofit organization the provided care for free to help the blind and visually impaired. This left Rev. Kim with the burden of constantly raising more money for the hospital to cover operating costs.

> *'If you can?' said Jesus. 'Everything is possible for him who believes.'*
> **Mark 9:23**

Rev. Suntae traveled all over Korea sharing his vision and testimony to promote the Siloam Eye Hospital and to collect donations for medical equipment. It was Chuseok, one of Korea's biggest national holidays, when Rev. Suntae Kim was about to fly to a church in Tokyo, Japan. Due to his busy schedule of fund-raising, Rev. Kim caught from a severe case of flu.

'I cannot stay in bed. I need to go to Japan to deliver the word of God. I need to get up.'

As soon as he tried to get up, his legs trembled and he had a splitting headache. He even heard a strange buzzing sound in his ears.

Suntae felt that he had no choice. He picked up his telephone to inform Tokyo Church the bad news that he would not be able to make his trip to Japan.

At that moment, he heard the voice of God saying, "Are you really a true servant of God? If you are, then, you should be able to sacrifice everything for the gospel even if it meant becoming a martyr."

"O, Lord, you are right. I was making excuses for myself because of physical pain, just like Jonah on his way to Tarshish. I will go to Japan even if it kills me."

Rev. Suntae cried sorrowfully holding the telephone in his hand.

'I almost forgot that God is sharing my pain with me. I will never forget that I will make any sacrifice for God and His work.'

Pastor Kim calmed himself down and headed to the airport.

"Lord, give me strength."

On his way in the airplane whenever he felt dizzy he prayed to God to give him strength to finish the mission entrusted to him.

O Lord, you have searched me and you know me. You know when I sit and when I rise; you perceive my thoughts from afar. You discern my going out and my lying down; you are familiar with all my ways. Before a word is on my tongue you know it completely, O Lord. You hem me in-behind and before; you have laid your hand upon me. Such knowledge is too wonderful for me, too lofty for me to attain. Where can I go from your Spirit? Where can I flee from your presence? If I go up to the heavens, you are there; if I make my bed in the depths, you are there. If I rise on the wings of the dawn, if I settle on the far side of the sea, even there your hand will guide me, your right hand will hold me fast. If I say, "Surely the darkness will hide me and the light becomes night around me," even the darkness will not be dark to you; the night will shine like the day, for darkness is as light to you. For you created my inmost being; you knit me together in my mother's womb. I praise you because I am fearfully and wonderfully made; your works are wonderful, I know that full well. My frame was not hidden from you when I was made in the secret place. When I was woven together in the depths of the earth, your eyes saw my unformed body. All the days ordained for me were written in your book before one of them came to be. How precious to me are your thoughts, O God! How vast is the sum of them! Were I to count them, they would outnumber the grains of sand. When I awake, I am still with you. If only you would slay the wicked, O God! Away from me, you bloodthirsty men! They speak of you with evil intent; your adversaries misuse your name. Do I not hate those who hate you, O Lord, and abhor those who rise up against you? I have nothing but hatred for them; I count them my enemies. Search me, O God, and know my heart; test me and know my anxious thoughts. See if there is any offensive way in me, and lead me in the way everlasting. **Psalm 139**

Many pastors were already waiting for Rev. Suntae at Narita airport.

"Why didn't you call us to say that you were sick and could not make it? How could you have come when you are so ill?"

"I was about to call but the Lord stopped me."

"God stopped you? This service will be blessed with God's special grace as you were to Tokyo by the will of God!"

Rev. Suntae was absolutely worn out after the morning and afternoon sermons. As he was resting in an office, one sister from the Tokyo Church came to visit him.

"Pastor, I came to see you to help support the Siloam Eye Hospital."

That sister carefully took out an envelope from her purse.

"It's not much money but I wish it could be of assistance to the Siloam Eye Hospital. If I have the chance, I would like to help more in the future."

In fact, there was huge amount of money in the envelope. Rev. Suntae could not hide his tears. He grasped her hands and express his gratitude to her and to God in prayer.

The sluggard craves and gets nothing, but the desires of the diligent are fully satisfied.   **Proverbs 13:4**

The Siloam Eye Hospital was built on the foundation of many people's prayers, dedication, and sacrifice. Today the Siloam Eye Hospital is continuously providing free eye treatment and eyesight recovery operations for those among the 200,000 blind and 5 million weak-sighted persons in danger of losing sight in South Korea.

But by the grace of God I am what I am, and his grace to me was not without effect. No, I worked harder than all of them-yet not I, but the grace of God that was with me.   **1 Corinthians 15:10**

Even today, the 70-year-old Rev. Suntae Kim still devotes his life to his his dreams and hopes for the visually impaired. Like the Apostle Paul, Rev. Suntae does not value wealth in this world, but rather longs for God's reward prepared in heaven.

The following hymn has become his favorite.

Who is on the Lord's side?
Who will serve the King?
Who will be His helpers, other lives to bring?
Who will leave the world's side?
Who will face the foe?
Who is on the Lord's side? Who for Him will go?
By Thy call of mercy, by Thy grace divine,
We are on the Lord's side — Savior, we are Thine!

Jesus, Thou hast bought us, not with gold or gem,
But with Thine own life blood, for Thy diadem;
With Thy blessing filling each who comes to Thee,
Thou hast made us willing,
Thou hast made us free.
By Thy grand redemption, by Thy grace divine,
We are on the Lord's side — Savior, we are Thine!

Rev. Suntae Kim believes that the world's best happiness is to give a hand to those in need and give them hope, comfort and assistance. Pastor Suntae Kim complete dedication to God and His calling has made it possible for him to receive the Ramon Magsaysay Award, referred to as 'the Nobel Prize of Asia.' Rev. Suntae donated all of his award money of 50,000 dollars toward the construction of a new facility called 'Siloam Eye Center.' Once, a long time ago, Rev. Suntae sincerely promised God that he would live giving away his possession to those in need. Even today Rev. Suntae still tries to keep that promise to God everyday.

"I used to be poor and miserable. As a young boy, I lost my parents, friends and even eyesight. I also lost my relatives, health, wealth and hope. Simply, I had lost all the basic things in life which most people are born with and cherish.

"However, I thank God for my difficult times. Since I had lost everything in my life, I was able to find heaven. If after I lost everything I had not become one seeking the one true God, whose hands reach down from high above, I would still be wandering around a beggar in this shallow, cruel world.

"Thanks to God's blessing, I realized that I should put my past behind me and not dwell on what I had lost. I resolved not to live as a foolish person in despair embittered by misfortune, but to look forward.

"Instead, I decided to become a new person who knows the increasing joys of storing up riches in heaven."

Part 5
Conclusion

Chapter 25
To Remain
a Deamer and a Boy

Suntae was an elementary school student when he read Helen Keller's biography for the first time. Helen Keller suffered from the multiple disabilities of blindness, deafness and a severe speech impediment. However, despite her disability she achieved three doctoral degrees, as well as, serving as a beacon of hope for the disabled around the world. Her miraculous story inspired little Suntae with hope and a dream.

On that day, after finishing her story, Suntae prayed.

"Heavenly Father, Helen Keller achieved three doctoral degrees in spite of her multiple disabilities. I think I am more fortunate than her as I can hear and talk. Please help me to study hard and become a great person like her."

Of course, Suntae's life from boyhood to being a pastor was a rocky road. Yet, he overcame all the obstacles through faith in God and prayer. At last, he accomplished his dream after sixty years of trials. Following in Helen Keller's footsteps, Suntae has achieved three doctoral degrees and was conferred the Magsaysay Award, known as Asia's Nobel Prize. Suntae's other dream was to teach those who wanted to become pastors like himself. God answered his prayers by allowing Suntae to become a professor at the seminary where he graduated from long ago.

Suntae wasn't satisfied with just that. He also founded several churches for the blind in Korea. And beyond that, he founded the Siloam Eye Hospital to help the blind and visually impaired restore their sight and receive proper medical care. That was not the end of his story. He established the 'Siloam Welfare Center for the Visually Impaired' to provide rehabilitation, job training, and education for daily life for those whom eye operations could not restore sight. His last dream that he prayed for finally came true when the Siloam Nursing Home for blind senior citizens was founded.

> *And it shall come to pass afterward, that I will pour out my spirit upon all flesh; and your sons and your daughters shall prophesy, your old men shall dream dreams, your young men shall see visions.*
>
> **Joel 2:28**

In his younger days whenever Suntae who had no parents or siblings was all alone in the empty school dormitory on every holiday and at vacations, he prayed for a family to go back to. He prayed for having his own happy family which would gather together, pray and praise God on every holiday. God in his grace listened to Suntae's prayer and blessed him with a loving family.

Just as he prayed, he met an excellent wife for his life who loves singing hymns to worship God. Like his wife, his two daughters majored in music and now he has a musical family. Pastor Suntae loves music and so he began the Siloam Eye Hospital Angel Voice Ensemble which he sometimes directed and played the accompaniment for to give glory and praise to God. So many times he shed tears in loneliness but God who saw the tears did not leave Suntae as a lonely orphan but always watched over him. Thus the innermost dreams which were as high as the heavens, and wide as the ocean all came to be fulfilled. Rev. Suntae Kim never ceases to help the blind, as it is his life's mission. In 2009, he established the Siloam Eye Center to provide eye treatment and operations for the visually impaired, starting in Korea but expanding his medical mission providing free treatment and eye operations to Asia, Africa, Central and Latin America. The center operates the Siloam Mobile Hospital, a 46-seat limousine bus with perfect medical equipment that travels even to remote areas and offers both daily and long-term treatment to those living in rural areas, islands, prisons, schools for the blind, and leper colonies throughout Korea. The traveling medical team gives free treatment to prevent the loss of sight and eye operations to heal and recover sight for the needy in poor areas and bring hope and the light of life for those in despair. With God's blessing, Suntae has three branches of his mission: the Siloam Eye Hospital, its global branches, and the Mobile Hospital. The Siloam hospitals provide eyesight recovery operations to bring a new light to many in darkness, as well as, providing free eye treatment preventing people from going blind. Suntae, who dreams and achieves many miracles, always says,

"Could I have achieved all of these things in my own strength? Not at all. God has supported me all along. And also the love, prayer and support of many persons have helped make all this possible. Love is great because it turns something impossible to the possible. We call this a 'miracle'."

Today Suntae is still dreaming. He dreams of expanding the nursing home to make more space for blind grandmothers and grandfathers who have nowhere to go so that they can spend the last moments of their life preparing for heaven. What he has in mind is to provide a shelter for the old and the sick in a beautiful sacred place like the Garden of Eden where the song of the birds is joined with hymn song and fruit trees bear their fruit in season. If someone asks Suntae "Are you still a dreamer?" Even ten years from today, his answer will definitely be "Yes!"

A Sermon

The Keys to Success in Life

A man needs assets and resources to run a business. Likewise, a man needs the same things to lead a fulfilling and fruitful life. What kind of assets and resources do we need to make a successful life? We need five assets:

The first asset is health. Health is the first and foremost resource. No matter how intelligent or virtuous you are, they are meaningless unless you are healthy. Health is like the cornerstone of life?it is the most fundamental and essential resource. Health is like air. We are not conscious of the presence of the air even though we are surrounded by it at all times. However, imagine if there wasn't any air, we would just simply die. Similarly, we don't recognize the importance of good health until we lose it. Again, Good health is the key to a happy life and it should be of primary concern. If you lose it, you lose everything.

The second asset is time. Life and time are inseparable. We live our lives based on so-called allotments of time. What does it mean if you are old? It means there isn't much time left to you. What does it mean if you are young? It means there is plenty of time available to you. Time is more valuable than gold. You can always buy gold somehow; however, it is impossible for you to buy time no matter how hard we may try. Spent time never returns. Once it fleets away, it is gone forever. Therefore, the biggest waste in life is to waste your precious time. You should be more careful about how you spend of your time than how you spend your money. Time is an evenly distributed asset to all the people in the world. The one who makes wise use of it can make a real success out of his or her life.

The third asset is knowledge. If you want to be economically independent, you absolutely need to possess knowledge of at least one special skill. We are living in modern society where labor has become highly divided and specialized. Without any special knowledge or skill, it is hard to get a job. In contrast, if you have special knowledge or skills, it is easy to survive in any culture and society. In other words if you don't have this asset in your life, you will fall behind and experience the sour taste of failure – so you should be prepared. Try hard to gain knowledge and skills, because knowledge is power.

Money is the fourth asset needed to live in comfort. However, you shouldn't put money above God. Money is just a means to an end. Although it is true that money is indispensable in your life, you shouldn't become a slave to money. The value of money reveals itself only when it is used in a good way.

Last but not least, morality and virtue is the fifth asset necessary to make a successful life. This asset is one of the most important of life's gifts. What is morality? It is an essential element you should equip yourself with to lead a virtuous life. It is comprised of loyalty, diligence, faith, conscience, responsibility and the spirit of cooperation and unity. These make a man more humane. To make the best use of four assets previously mentioned—health, time, knowledge and money—you need to keep morality and virtue in mind above all things. You should try to keep studying and learning to attain morality and virtue because, like I told you before, it is the most crucial possession in your life.

Beside these five assets, there are also three types of liquid we need in life: First, you need to sweat. Sweat is of great importance to a person. The original sin of Adam and Eve resulted in mankind having to sweat to make a living. Most people are indisposed and unwilling to sweat by nature. However, sweating is very important? it is a symbol of hard work and diligence. The knowledge and mind we have cultivated by virtue of many years of hard work and sweat is priceless. The success and happiness we achieve in life is paid for in sweat.

Although I am blind, for my junior high and high school education, I didn't go a blind school but chose to study the regular curriculum. I graduated from a regular middle school, high school, university, graduate school, and theological seminary. When I was a middle school and high school student, we were all poor. The Korean educational system couldn't afford to meet the basic needs of ordinary students, let alone of visually challenged students like myself. You can't even imagine how painful it was for me to study without books in Braille. I had to climb 380 stairs to go to school everyday with a schoolbag in one hand and a typewriter in the other. I felt sweat drench my entire body each time I had to climb the 380 stairs of our school. But for all the obstacles and difficulties I had to encounter, I worked hard and persevered. My sweat is what made me a leader. It is allowed me to do imposible things and has even allow me receive the Magsaysay Award. Young boys and girls! If you are eager to become successful in life, my simple advice to you is: "sweat!" Do your utmost devoting all your energy until you perspire. Success is only built on hard work and sweat.

The second vital liquid is tears. What lesson do tears teach us? Tears are not only the symbol of love but also the symbol of sincerity. As you all know, Helen Keller was born with three disabilities: She couldn't see, hear or speak. Her dedicated mother prayed for her more than an hour and a half everyday. She loved her daughter and devoted her tears to her daughter's success. Helen Keller's teacher, Anne Sullivan also gave her tireless effort and sincere love. Thanks to the tears of her mother and teacher, the poor girl was able to become one of the greatest and happiest people in the world. If you dedicate your tears to your suffering neighbor, I guarantee you will be filled with satisfaction and happiness.

The last liquid necessary in our lives is blood. What is the meaning of blood? It signifies life. In other words it is martyrdom. If you pray and strive with a spirit of sacrifice in your life, without a doubt you will achieve success. I hope that you young people can live a happy and successful life through faith and sacrifice. Value the assets of your life—health, time, knowledge, money and morality—and invest your sweat, tears and blood. If you do as much, your life will bring you not only success, but also great satisfaction and meaning.

Poems

If Only I Could See Again

If only I could see again,
I want to become a pilot and fly high above in the sky.

If only I could see again,
I want to fly across the wide Pacific.

If only I could see again,
I want to drive down the highway from Seoul to Busan,

Seeing the mountains rivers, and the
Beautiful, bountiful fruit ripening on trees.

If only I could see again,
I want to appreciate yellow and silver fields of grain
Ripening under the autumn sunshine.

If only I could see again
I want to jump, hop,
Play basketball, football, and volleyball,
Just as I wanted to do as a child
While watching my friends playing with balls.

How thrilled I would be
If only that day would come for real
But now, I am happy as I am.

Faces I Want to See

One autumn day
I went home from my day's work
And prayed on my knees.

"Thank you God for guiding me as always."
I changed into comfortable clothes
And sat around with my family over dinner.

My first daughter, Eunhye asked me,
"Daddy, can you really not see the world?"
My second daughter, Jihye asked the same, "Can't you?"
I answered, "I cannot see the sunlight as well as the fire light."

They asked again, "Then you have no idea
How Mom or we children look like, do you?"

I answered, "I cannot see you with my own eyes
But I can see you with the eyes of my heart."

"Dad, you want to see Mom and us
With your own eyes someday, right?"

Then, I couldn't stop from bursting into tears.
Yes, I don't know the faces of my family,
But I didn't want to show them how sad I was.
My answer was sad enough already,
And my tears would only bring my family more pain.

So I walked into my room and thought,
'Will the day come when I regain my eyesight
To see my wife and two daughters?'

Although it was a long while ago,
Yet still that evening is fresh in my mind.
I long to see my wife, two daughters, and my first granddaughter.

As I cannot see them,
I love my family even more.
God, bless my family!

The Horrifying War

Bang! Bang! Bang! Bang! Bang!
Bullets are pouring from the sky like rain
Everywhere airplanes pass attacking.

Mom, Mom! Help me!
I can hear the Sound of babies crying.

People are dying in pain
Mothers are running away
Leaving their babies behind
Children are wandering around
Looking for their family members
Those crying out in tears for their mother's milk or rice
And people fallen for lack of food.

Bang! Bang! Bang! Bang! Bang!
Houses are burning on fire from the bullets
A red sea of fire blazes up.
Refugees are heading southward, southward
With heavy bundles on their backs

Boom!
Seoul's Han River Bridge is blown apart.
Unaware,
People were crossing the bridge.
People drown in the river
Clutching their babies and bundles.
Also North Korean soldiers
Kill innocent civilians.

People lost eyes
Lost arms
Lost legs
Lost lives
Leaving only bloody screams

I saw everything.
In 1950
The tragedy of the Korean War.
War is horrifying.
War is a disaster for mankind.
History should not repeat itself again.

The only thing war left:
Death
And innocent people who lost their eyes, arms and legs
Dead bodies of people shot by guns,
Too many to count, lying everywhere
War is a miserable painful tragedy
For all humanity.

If Only I Had Had a Little More Money

I was a poor kid.
The things I dreamt about were not mine.

If only I had had a little more money
I would have learned cello, and violin.
With beautiful melodies I would play
I wanted to worship God, Creator of all.

If only I had a little more money
I would have become a cellist, pianist, or violinist.
With beautiful melodies I would play,
I wanted to travel around the world,
Giving hope to people in despair and sorrow.

If only I had had a little more money
I would have become a great person.
I wanted to study with a tutor like others do,
Science, art, and all the school subjects.

I was sad and I was upset
But I prayed
Two meals a day were all I had
But I had a heart full of hope.

Every time I was lost in despair
God told me, 'Don't worry Suntae.
I will take care of you.'

With all those dark hard days all behind me
By God's will and grace
I'm said to be a helper for those whose eyes and hearts
Are in the dark and despair.

The Boy
in Search
of Heaven's
Light

Ways to Support the Siloam Eye Hospital

All proceeds of this book go to support the work of the Siloam Eye Hospital founded by Rev. Suntae Kim. If you would like to order more copies for your friends please let us know by email or letter to the following address:

> Siloam Eye Hospital
> **181 Deung Chon-No,**
> **Gang Seo-Gu,**
> **Seoul South Korea 157-836**
> **Tel : +82-2-2650-0700**
>
> **email : eyesight@siloam.co.kr**

"I hope you will view our work meaningful and that you become a lasting contributor and partner of the Siloam Eye Hospital. I humbly ask that you might support us through your prayers and financial donations, as it is only with the support of people like you around the world that we are able to continue this great work of helping our brothers and sisters suffering in darkness. I ask that you might remember the important work God has entrusted to us and keep us in your prayers! Jesus said, 'Whatever you did for the least of My brothers and sisters, you did for Me'".

Rev. Suntae Kim

If you would like more information about the work of the Siloam Eye Hospital please refer to our website: www.siloam.co.kr.

Those of you who were moved by Rev. Kim's story and would like to make a monetary contribution to the work of the Siloam Eye Hospital can donate through the following banks:

> Korea:
> **Hana Bank**
> **Account Name: Siloam Eye Hospital**
> **Account #: 556-810018-37305**
>
> United States:
> **Shinhan Bank America, (Olympic Blvd. L.A.)**
> **Account Name: Siloam Mission Support in America**
> **Account #: 7000-0023-0990**

Word of Life Press

Mission Statement
"So that you will prove yourselves to be blameless and innocent, children of God above reproach in the midst of a crooked and perverse generation, among whom you appear as lights in the world, holding fast the word of life, so that in the day of Christ I will have reason to glory because I did not run in vain nor toil in vain."

(Philippians 2:15-16)

We will reveal the life of God.
We will reveal the life that Jesus has given to us in every one of our printed books
to deliver the gospel of Jesus.
We will deliver the Word of God.
We will contribute to growing the church by delivering God's message, the source of life.
We will light the world.
We will publish books that light the darkness
and lead us to God.
We will act with purity.
We will put honesty into practice in the publishing of books and management of our business.
We will always spread gospel.
We will carry out our mission of spreading the gospel to everyone, everywhere,
till the time when our Lord returns to save us.

GwangHwaMun, Seoul
110-061 58-1 2F. Salvation Army Hall, Sinmunno 1-ga, Jongno-gu, Seoul, Korea
TEL (02) 737-2288   FAX (02) 737-4623

GangNam, Seoul
137-909 75-19 2F. Banpo Shopping Town 3, Jamwon-dong, Seocho-gu, Seoul, Korea
TEL (02) 858-8744   FAX (02) 595-3549

Guro, Seoul
152-880 1123-1 3F. Guro 3-dong, Guro-gu, Seoul, Korea
TEL (02) 858-8744   FAX (02) 838-0653

Nowon, Seoul
139-200 749-4 B1. Sambong Building, Sanggye-dong, Nowon-gu, Seoul, Korea
TEL (02) 938-7979   FAX (02) 3391-6169

Bundang, Gyeonggi-do
463-824 269-5 4F. Seowon Plaza, Seohyeon Bookstore, Seohyeon-dong, Bundang-gu, Seongnam-si, Gyeonggi-do, Korea
TEL (031) 707-5566   FAX (031) 707-4999

Sincheon, Seoul
121-806 107-1, 8F. Dongin Building, Nogosan-dong, Mapo-gu, Seoul, Korea
TEL (02) 702-1411   FAX (02) 702-1131

Ilsan, Gyeonggi-do
411-370 83 B1. Laketown, Juyeop-dong, Ilsanseo-gu, Goyang-si, Gyeonggi-do, Korea
TEL (031) 916-8787   FAX (031) 916-8788

Uijeongbu-si. Gyeonggi-do
484-010 470-4 3F, Sungsan Tower, Geumo-dong, Uijeongbu-si, Gyeonggi-do, Korea
TEL (031) 845-0600   FAX (031) 852-6930

Online bookstore
http:/www.lifebook.co.kr